CW00858046

UNTIL *Death* DO WE *Meet*

A Focus Heavenward Book

Sharyn M. Balogh

WESTBOW
PRESS®
A DIVISION OF THOMAS NELSON
& ZONDERVAN

WestBow Press books may be ordered through booksellers or by contacting:

WestBow Press
A Division of Thomas Nelson & Zondervan
1663 Liberty Drive
Bloomington, IN 47403
www.westbowpress.com
1 (866) 928-1240

Cover illustration by Aimee Michele Reyes, 2019.

All Scripture quotations are taken from The New American Standard Bible®, Copyright © 1960, 1962, 1963, 1968, 1971, 1972, 1973, 1975, 1977, 1995 by The Lockman Foundation. Used by permission.

ISBN: 978-1-9736-6024-8 (sc)
ISBN: 978-1-9736-6023-1 (hc)
ISBN: 978-1-9736-6025-5 (e)

Library of Congress Control Number: 2019904406

Print information available on the last page.

WestBow Press rev. date: 6/3/2019

CONTENTS

Acknowledgements ix

Introduction xi

Chapter 1   The Proposal and Acceptance: Getting to
Know You 1

Chapter 2   To Have and to Hold 13

Chapter 3   For Better or for Worse 21

Chapter 4   For Richer, for Poorer 33

Chapter 5   In Sickness and in Health 47

Chapter 6   Hand in Hand 59

Chapter 7   Purity and Devotion 69

Chapter 8   Face-to-Face 83

To My Children

Daniel Joseph Scott
Kevin Robert Scott
Aimee Michele Reyes

ACKNOWLEDGEMENTS

I am gratefully and forever, by choice and by His choosing, indebted to my Savior and Lord Jesus Christ. Forever my life is changed, my heart has been transplanted with His love. God, in His grace, has placed countless individuals around me who have encouraged me and challenged me to grow in my love for Christ. Dale and Lynn Whitehead, thank you for taking me under the wings of your care and instruction so many years ago, you are faithful and treasured friends. Since the transformation of my heart through God's touch, I have been surrounded by love and support at Valley Bible Church. Cindy Rantal, thank you for reminding me early in my walk that God was always to be what I was striving for in the desires of my heart. To my sweet neighbor of long ago, Lois Brasile, thank you for being constantly available to watch my children when I was a single mom, and teaching me by example to share the gospel with all who would listen. I could never include all those who have willingly invested in my life, always pointing me toward God. Thank you Katie Scott, one of my sweet daughter-in-laws, who first encouraged me to start publishing my studies in a blog – even knowing I was somewhat electronically challenged – look at what you started, who knew! I am always and forever blessed by my three children who have weathered the storms with me and welcomed with open arms a most special gift in our lives - my husband Rick – the one they call Dad, almost three decades ago. Rick jumped into our broken family, completely accepted three young children as his own and provided an excellent example of faith and commitment for us to follow. He has tirelessly read and re-read every word I have put to paper, checking for accuracy, clarity, and correct interpretation, always encouraging me to keep on keeping on as my desire to write and speak of God's wonder has increased. Thank you Lord for showering your blessings upon me through those who love You.

INTRODUCTION

He Loves Me!

P romises, contracts, oaths, vows—these are all different signs of commitment. We promise to do something, we put our signatures on contracts to secure expectations of the parties involved, we take oaths to uphold certain agreed-upon values, and we show the sincerity of our commitment in spoken vows to one another.

Yet are we truly able to keep all of our promises, fulfill every contract perfectly, maintain each word of an oath we have recited with absolute completeness, and carry out each part of a vow with success?

Our answer—probably not. The truth—most definitely not! Each of our relationships is dependent on a certain fulfillment of spoken and unspoken expectations. If we were able to always say and do everything perfectly, there would be no problems with commitment. And many lawyers would be out of a job!

But we have a great deal of hope! Relationships can and do work. And they work well when they are based on the truths of God's love for us. When we begin to understand God's love and commitment to us, what He has done for us, and what He expects of us, each of our personal relationships with friends, families, spouses, neighbors, and colleagues will be affected for the better.

Keep in mind as you read this book that the most important application to make is your own personal response to God's love and commitment toward you. So although there will be reference to a marriage relationship, this is not the major inference.

I pray you will recognize that a greater appreciation of God's faithfulness toward His children produces a desire to extend that same faithfulness and devotion toward the individuals He has placed in your life.

Traditional wedding vows have been used for centuries. The oldest traditional wedding vows have been traced back to the manuals of the medieval church. Nearly everyone would agree that at a wedding ceremony itself, the most anticipated, romantic, and emotional part of the entire function is when the bride and groom gaze into each other's eyes and pledge their undying love as they recite their vows to each other.

Typically, in these vows, the bride and groom will express their feelings toward each other and promise to stay true through the good, the bad, and the ugly. As the couple hold hands and lovingly look at each other, they wholeheartedly believe that the person staring back at them is their true soul mate, the only one for them forever. Certainly, there is nothing that will ever come between them or cause them to feel different. Except, of course, death.

Perhaps this familiar setting conjures up memories you have of your own special day. Those memories may be wonderful or they may feel bittersweet. Nonetheless, every reader can relate in some way to this scenario of two people professing their faithfulness until death. Often, I will have an invitation or announcement for a wedding on my desk. Something new in the last decade or so is the practice of sending out save-the-date cards. I actually appreciate these advance notices, so I can be sure to put the date on my calendar!

Try as you might, you will not find what the population considers traditional wedding vows in the Bible. However, there are references to marriage. Beginning in Genesis 2:24, it says, "Therefore shall a man leave his father and his mother, and shall cleave unto his wife: and they shall be one flesh." Marriage was intended by God for man so that he would not be alone (Genesis 2:18) and for the purpose of populating the world (Genesis 1:28).

A vow of marriage was considered a contract only ending when one partner dies (1 Corinthians 7:39). The ending proclamation in many traditional wedding ceremonies just prior to announcing the bride and groom as Mr. and Mrs. comes from Matthew 19:6, which says, "What therefore God has joined together, let no man separate."

Although you will not find a list of vows to recite at a wedding in the Bible, you can see that some of our traditionally based ceremony comes from God's Word.

Yet when we strip all the convention away, the vow of marriage is simply a civil union that two people enter into willingly. It is marked by satisfactory adherence of two individuals conducting themselves according to an agreed-upon contract. It is legal and binding. You may cringe at the word *satisfactory* used above, but the reality is we aren't perfect. Therefore even an exceptional spouse will only be able to fulfill every expectation some of the time. Even in our best efforts we fail; hence, forgiveness is a necessary and huge component in a successful marriage between two individuals.

A marriage contract can be entered into with a quick court appearance before a judge. Or, if preferred, a ceremony may be planned to make a union known publicly, and it can be as varied as there are peoples and customs. The ceremony might be simple with a cake-and-punch reception afterward, or it might be an elaborate event with a full meal, announcements, music, and celebration into the night.

The word *wedding* comes from an Old English word *wedd*, which means to wager or to redeem a pledge. On an interesting note, when you consider the word *wager*, it is regarded as an act of gambling, as in making a bet on how something will turn out. This idea unfortunately seems to fit some thinking of our modern society today. Using the word *pledge* at least would imply a promise to seriously try to adhere to the commitment that was made. Notice the definition above of the original English word: to redeem a pledge. Now consider the illustration of God's union with the Jewish nation. Read Isaiah 54:5: "For your husband is your Maker, Whose name is the LORD of hosts; and your Redeemer is the Holy One of Israel, Who is called the God of all the earth."

God has redeemed humankind through His Son, Jesus Christ. Jesus's life, death, and resurrection were needed to restore humankind. Our Redeemer, Jesus Christ, ransomed us from the bondage of sin. Our value lies in this redemption. Our worth lies in God's plan to pledge His Son as the payment for sin.

Although the format of traditional wedding vows is referenced in this book, this material is not meant to be used solely for a marriage relationship. God's promises to us, once understood and accepted, will change our devotion to Him. Our relationship with Him is built upon His mercy and grace.

As you read you will find definite application to a wedded union and also purposeful application for all who have received

God's eternal promise to them. The truths of God's devotion will affect every relationship you have, but most importantly your relationship with God will grow as you understand His love for you in a more direct and personal way.

Seriously consider what He offers and why you should accept His proposal. As you read through the wording of vows that resonate in a familiar setting, you will discover God's promises to His children now and into eternity.

Since the Bible refers to Christ often as a bridegroom and His church as the bride, it seems appropriate to take an opportunity to use something familiar and apply it to our relationship with the Savior of humankind, Jesus Christ.

As you read, I pray you are encouraged, challenged, and fall in love even more with your Savior. Since it is God's Word that we hold on to, several scripture references are included in this book for you to ponder. My strength is not biblical theology, but I have tried my best to represent the verses used in their correct context and setting. This book is meant to draw you into your own personal study of scripture as you look up references and consider the questions presented. All scripture is taken from the New American Standard version of the Bible unless otherwise noted.

Read what Paul says to the Corinthian church in 2 Corinthians 11:2: "For I am jealous for you with a godly jealousy; for I betrothed you to one husband, that to Christ I might present you as a pure virgin." Paul desires the believers in Corinth to present themselves fully devoted to God.

This same picture of a bride adorned for her husband is seen in the book of Revelation. Chapter 21:2 states, "And I saw the holy city, new Jerusalem, coming down out of heaven from God, made ready as a bride adorned for her husband."

Also, take a look at Revelation 21:9: "And one of the seven angels who had the seven bowls full of the seven last plagues, came and spoke with me, saying, 'Come here, I shall show you the bride, the wife of the Lamb.'"

In Isaiah 62, we read of God's design for the church. Isaiah 62:4–5 states, "It will no longer be said to you, 'Forsaken,' nor to your land will it any longer be said, 'Desolate'; But you will be called, 'My delight is in her,' and your land, 'Married'; For the LORD delights in you, and [to Him] your land will be married. For [as] a young man marries a virgin, [So] your sons will marry you; and [as] the bridegroom rejoices over the bride, [So] your God will rejoice over you."

Interspersed throughout this book are important questions for you to consider. I suggest taking the time to thoughtfully and truthfully ponder your answers. As God speaks to you through His Word, may you see more clearly the design He has for His children. I pray you look forward to that day when you will meet Him face-to-face, adorned with the holiness that comes from Jesus.

CHAPTER 1

The Proposal and Acceptance: Getting to Know You

I Confess You to Be My Savior and Lord …

B efore most weddings there is an intention stated—a proposal where the plan or goals for the future are discussed and understood. Usually two people have spent some time getting to know each other. We call this dating. Several generations ago, the term *courting* was used to describe this romantic relationship where two individuals meet regularly, usually with the thought of marriage in the future. When dating someone, the immediate purpose is to have opportunities to ask questions, observe behavior in different situations, and discover more about the history of the person. Learning someone's likes and dislikes, what pleases him or her, and what his or her goals are gives you important information of the person's expectations and plans for the future.

Let us look at who Jesus is so we can seriously regard God's proposal to us. The first chapter of the book of John tells us Jesus is Creator; He is eternal; He is the true Light; He became flesh and dwelled among us; He is the only begotten Son of God; grace and truth are realized through Him; Jesus is Lord, the Lamb of God who takes away the sin of the world; He is our Teacher; the Messiah; the King of Israel; and the Son of man (John 1:1–51).

This list is just from one chapter out of one book in the Bible!

Consider this: When you have an important decision to make, what do you do? What are the facts you study?

My husband and I reach most major decisions painfully slow. We gather information and typically ask lots of questions. When we have purchased vehicles, we've searched reports and looked at ratings; when our children each went to college, we visited the universities and asked about the percentage of students who graduated and the background of professors teaching. We have searched the internet for statements of beliefs when helping our children find a church in their college towns. A few years ago, we decided to purchase a new coffee maker and yes, we both researched different brands and the positives and negatives, along with the price-for-value ratings. We are very pleased with the one we bought!

Think about medical treatments for a moment. Most of us would not consider going to a doctor who did not have the proper credentials. If a serious problem were discovered, we would get a second or even a third opinion to be sure we have all the correct information.

Keep in mind the tremendous information, or credentials, listed earlier in the Bible about who Jesus is, and let us also look at what He did.

Jesus voluntarily gave His life for ours. Let that truth sink in for a moment. Did you ask Jesus to give His life so you could live? I seriously doubt we would be humble enough to do this. On what merit would we deserve such a gift?

John 10:14–15 says, "I am the good shepherd; and I know My own, and My own know Me, even as the Father knows Me and I know the Father; and I lay down My life for the sheep."

Jesus is perfect yet accepted punishment for the sin of the entire world so that we might have eternal life. Jesus, our Creator, the Son of God, our Lord, Teacher, Messiah, and King, humbled Himself to a physical, horrific death on a cross because He loves us that much—more than we will ever be able to comprehend. Jesus voluntarily died for us. He was not guilty, not even just a little bit. He was perfect. He did not owe the punishment for sin that is ours to bear, yet in obedience to His Father and because of His incomprehensible love, we are free from the penalty of sin. John 3:16 is a verse many people have heard, but what is your understanding of it?

John 3:16 reads, "For God so loved the world that He gave His only begotten Son, that whoever believes in Him should not perish, but have eternal life."

God (remember the description of Him listed earlier) so loved the world—us, the world's inhabitants, His created people—that He gave Jesus as His gift of reconciliation, even knowing that Jesus would suffer and die. Why? So that we might not be punished for our sins. So that we would have everlasting life. This kind of love is mind-boggling. I personally cannot conceive of giving one of my children over to be sacrificed for someone else's wrongdoing, can you?

When we begin to appreciate even just a portion of the information written down for us in the Bible about who Christ is and what He did, it is truly baffling to think He would even know our names let alone offer us anything. He is King of the world. All I bring to the table is my sin and need of a Savior. God does everything else.

God does have a serious proposal for us, and it is important that we understand His plan, the gospel. My husband is an educator and enjoyed teaching at our local community college for nearly four decades. One the most compelling reasons for his success as a teacher is his understanding that you only grasp something when you can turn around and explain it to someone else.

The Bible says God wants us for Himself. He wants a relationship with us. He prefers us above all other creation. God has made a deliberate decision that we are the most suitable to live eternally with Him.

In 2 Thessalonians 2:13, it says, "But we should always give thanks to God for you, brethren beloved by the Lord, because God has chosen you from the beginning for salvation through sanctification by the Spirit and faith in the truth."

How can that be? This is like winning the lottery without even playing it! I have not even invested any personal resources in this plan. I am sure we cannot fully comprehend all the implications of God's love for us and how He chose us. But we do have enough information to make an appropriate decision of whether we'll accept His gift or not.

God's Word explains that heaven is a free gift. All true gifts are free. Hopefully, the gifts you choose to give others are done so without an expectation of return. If you look up the definition of gift, you will find that it is something acquired without compensation.

Heaven is not something we can work hard for, check all the boxes, and obtain. It is also not something we deserve on our own merit. Two familiar verses that come to mind are found in the books of Romans and Ephesians. Romans 6:23 says, "For the wages of sin is death, but the free gift of God is eternal life in Christ Jesus our Lord." And in Ephesians 2:8–9, we read, "For by grace you have been saved through faith; and that not of yourselves, [it is] the gift of God; not as a result of works, that no one should boast."

We are not only unable to earn the gift of heaven, we are sinners and there is a penalty owed for our transgressions that we are unable to pay. Before you think to yourself, *I am not that bad,* or *I have not committed any grievous sin"*, remember all it takes is one sin to be blemished. God's standard is perfection because He is perfect. Even one unkind thought causes us to be imperfect.

Several weeks ago, I bought a bag of oranges from a major wholesale chain. I was in a hurry and did not notice the moldy orange toward the bottom of the bag until I got home. I would have put that bag aside in the store had I realized when I was there that it had a bad piece of fruit in it. Even though the other oranges looked fine, that one bad one tainted the entire bag.

God loves us, but since He is perfect, He cannot look upon our sin. His perfect character is unable to abide in the presence of sin. As a result of our sin, our relationship with God has been severed. There's a chasm between us that we are unable to cross. God desires to be with us, and we need to be saved so we can be with Him! We need a Savior to make things right. God sent His perfect Son, Jesus, to be our perfect sacrifice. Only through Jesus can we be saved.

In the book of John, when Thomas asked how he and the other disciples would know the way to go, Jesus replied, "I am the way, and the truth, and the life; no one comes to the Father, but through Me" (John 14:6).

Consider God's Son, Jesus. Perfect in all ways. Given to us to die sacrificially on a cross.

Through Jesus's death, the payment for our sin and the sin of the entire world was fully covered. The chasm separating us from God has been bridged by His Son's death and resurrection.

Traditional wedding vows begin with the words "I take you." Since the essential plan of salvation and the choosing of it originates from God and is completed in His Son, we'll change the wording to "I confess." To confess something means we admit to the truth. Specifically, in this context, we admit that we need to be saved from the penalty of our sin. This is the first step in our relationship with Christ.

I confess You, Jesus Christ, to be my Savior and Lord.

Romans 10:9–10 says that "if you confess with your mouth Jesus [as] Lord, and believe in your heart that God raised Him from the dead, you shall be saved; for with the heart man believes, resulting in righteousness, and with the mouth he confesses, resulting in salvation."

Our acceptance of the gift of salvation is a declaration that what God says is true. He says we are sinful, and we wholeheartedly agree. He says we need His Son to save us, and we say amen! We then accept His plan and enter into a covenant with Him.

Recognize at the beginning of most wedding vows there is a question asked of each participant. It is worded something like this: "Do you, (insert name here), take (insert another name here), to be your lawfully wedded husband/wife." At this time, each partner has the opportunity to say, "I do."

God asks each of us to accept His Son as our Lord and Savior. However, we are not forced into this agreement, just as two people are not or should not be forced into marriage. Salvation is available to each of us but must be accepted not only with an understanding of our minds but most important, with our hearts—recognizing the need we have for a Savior.

The action of accepting God's proposal is available only through His grace. God opens our eyes to the truth and allows us to respond favorably. Our response should be accompanied by a sincere desire to worship and follow God. John 10:27 says, "My sheep hear My voice, and I know them, and they follow Me."

I have three brothers, two older and one who is four years younger. I remember sitting with my younger brother in the kitchen after everyone else in our family was finished with dinner. He was always much more interested in the things going on around him than he was in eating. While my mom washed the dishes, I would try all kinds of things to get my brother to finish his dinner. I'm sure some of you can relate to this with stories of your own. Have you ever played airplane with a spoonful of food? How about choo-choo? "Here comes the train; open the tunnel!" Quite a bit of effort went into persuading my little brother to eat so he would grow up healthy and strong.

If you have animals as pets, you know what it's like to get your dog or cat to swallow a pill. We used to have a basset hound named Barnie Belle—not real smart but cute and definitely stubborn! To get her to take medication, my husband would literally shove a tablet into the back of her throat, hold her mouth closed, and quickly blow in her face. No matter how many times this happened, she was surprised and would swallow!

Our son's dog, Pooh Bear, would take medication without a problem, as long as it was disguised and wrapped in a piece of bologna. The worst one was Squirt, my daughter's cat. In order to get her to swallow a pill, you would have to force your finger halfway down her throat while trying to hold on to her—not a pretty picture!

We were not thrilled to go through the process of giving our dogs and cat medications, yet we were willing to take whatever action was necessary because we loved our pets.

God loves us and knows what we need. He took extreme measures to save us from sin and redeem us for Himself. He knows what is best for us and desires each of us to escape the judgment of hell we deserve. He has given us the remedy. Unlike the games used to get my brother to eat or the trickery and coercion used to give our animals medication, God will not force us to accept His plan. His gift of salvation is the only thing that will keep us

7

from spiritual death and eternal condemnation, but He will not make us receive His gift. He will not shove it down our throats like a pill we need or disguise it as something else. Through His grace, we must freely accept what He offers. God does not play games with us.

God has offered to us His plan of redemption through Jesus. We need to respond. Each individual reading this has either accepted or rejected Christ. There is no middle road. You may be thinking this is not the right time or perhaps it's something to consider at a later date. Perhaps you believe God is right for someone else but not necessary for you. At one point, either now or in the future, you will have to make a choice. Just as we cannot drive down a road for very long without eventually having to turn right or left, we are unable to ignore Christ's proposal forever.

You may even think of several reasonable arguments to not apply Christ's proposal to yourself personally. It may not seem fair that people die or that they suffer. It may be difficult to understand why we see evil around us.

You may not be able to accept the hypocrisy you have seen demonstrated in those who say they are Christians. You do not need to worry about everyone else. God knows all, and He will take care of things in His perfect time. The only one you are accountable for is yourself. The one you will be held accountable to is God. Have you accepted Christ's proposal and gift of eternal life?

Often a beautiful ring is given upon the acceptance of a wedding proposal. It symbolizes a promise for the future and is proudly worn for everyone to see. God gives to us the gift of His Holy Spirit when we accept Jesus. The Holy Spirit is Jesus's promise to us for the future we have with Him. 2 Corinthians 1:22 says that God "sealed us and gave us the Spirit in our hearts as a pledge." What we need to do is place our hands in His outstretched arms and reach out to receive the gift He offers.

What usually follows the acceptance of a proposal? Great excitement! You simply cannot wait to tell everyone all the details! My husband asked me to marry him late in the evening, and I remember calling my family and a few close friends at two in the morning to share the news!

When we are truly excited and believe strongly in something or someone, we have a difficult time being quiet! More than three decades ago, the church I attend was quite a bit smaller and the music was a bit less formal. We used to sing a song that began with the words "shake a friend's hand." Depending on who was leading music, the words would be replaced by different actions, basically meant to give us time to greet one another. At this time, we would not only shake a friend's hand but also pat a friend's back and even sometimes squeeze a friend's knee.

This song was always fun and a great way to start a service. The Sunday after I was engaged, a close friend was leading music and began with the song I just described. After a few of the usual verses, he sang the words "check a friend's ring." Of course everyone was happy to share in the news of our engagement!

When we understand the gift we've been given in Christ, there is nothing we would rather discuss with those around us. We are compelled to speak about His love.

When I was eighteen years old, I worked in a physician's office. I remember a young woman in her early twenties who answered the phones. I was very uncomfortable around her. It's not because she wasn't nice; she was probably the most thoughtful, honest, and kind employee in the office. But almost every time we had a conversation, it would center on God, her church, and her involvement at her church, resulting in an invitation to attend. She even asked me to go to a Bible study with her. I remember thinking to myself that she was like one of those evangelist people I had heard about— the ones who would knock on your door and try to talk to you about the Bible. Can you imagine?

I was not very welcoming toward her friendship, and regrettably, I do not even recall her name. But if I could, I would thank her for trying to share with me what was vitally important. Regardless of the reception she received from those around her, she couldn't stop talking about her commitment to Christ. God bless her heart for living out the gospel. By the way, about those evangelist people who try to talk about God, I've knocked on a few doors myself since then! God has a wonderful sense of humor as He unfolds His perfect plan!

If you have accepted the proposal of eternal life Christ has offered, get excited! Speak boldly of what God has done in your life! It will remind you of the amazing gift you have received, and it will encourage others to remember their commitment also.

If you have not acknowledged your need for a Savior, there is no time like now. Simply confess your sin and accept Jesus's death on the cross for you. Let God know you desire to follow Him in obedience. Tell Him you recognize your need to be saved from a sinful, selfish world that has no hope for the future. Then let those around you rejoice with you in your commitment to Christ. Get excited because your life will forever be changed, even into eternity!

Just as a wedding proposal points us toward that special day when two people are united, Christ's proposal to us, once accepted, shifts our focus from things of this earth toward the riches of heaven. We have a future full of promise and certainty!

Metaphorically, Christ is our bridegroom and the church is His bride. This relationship signifies the necessity of our complete devotion to Him. In this relationship, we are promised His continual care.

Revelation 19:7 says, "Let us rejoice and be glad and give the glory to Him, for the marriage of the Lamb has come and His bride has made herself ready."

If you're like me, you may feel that you do not understand much of the theology contained in God's Word, but certainly we can see the relationship between ourselves and Christ as one that betroths us to Him as His children. When a bride is promised to her betrothed, there is an expectation of his care and protection. In our relationship with Christ, He becomes the head, the protector, the provider, the one for whom we are intended. We then seek to adorn ourselves in our best attire, to be made ready for this eternal union.

I encourage you to look at your attire—what you are putting on, and what you are seeking to put away regarding Christ—as you contemplate these words.

CHAPTER

2

To Have and to Hold

To Have and to Hold from This Day Forward

After the proposal offered to us in Christ through His death and resurrection, we are connected to all God's blessings. In chapter one, the familiar words in the pattern of wedding vows, "I take you to be my lawfully wedded husband/wife," were replaced by "I confess you Jesus as Lord and Savior." The word *confess* means to admit to the truth, specifically in the context of our sin.

Now, think upon what it means "to have or to hold from this day forward." To say the words "I have a car" conveys the understanding that you have a vehicle accessible for your use. Or consider this thought: many individuals have varying degrees of education. They have in their possession something that shows they have done what is required to receive a certificate of completion.

Holding something means nearly the same thing as above yet with an emphasis on maintaining it, such as "holding a thought." It can also mean to carry, to grasp, and to guard. When you hold up something, you keep it or support it. Think of holding up the garage door when the track system fails! *Sustain* is an appropriate synonym for hold.

Most traditional wedding vows begin with the formal question, "Do you take (insert name) to be your lawfully wedded husband/wife?" The next line begins an introduction of what this commitment might mean in several different life scenarios.

"To have and to hold from this day forward" - these words add permanence to our covenant. It is a statement of possession. It is a statement of forever. Yet, in human thinking, forever is subjective. How many individuals have seen love come and go? Perhaps numerous times? Unfortunately, there are many broken hearts represented all around us, either through death, divorce, or even simple misunderstandings.

There is good news: God's love will never change and will never end. It is certain, guaranteed, absolute, definite, assured, and dependable! God is eternal. There is nothing you can do to change His mind about His love for you. There can be no irreconcilable differences. God perfectly understands your heart, and He is patient with you as your understanding of Him increases.

God's forever is very different than the world's forever. The phrase "from this day forward" lasts through eternity!

We use phrases like "I will love you forever," and the words *always* and *promise* are used with almost a blasé attitude. What we mean is we'll hold on to that thought until a better person or thing comes along. The world's meaning of forever is not the same as God's. God's forever is eternal, from the beginning of time, and without end.

There are several references to God's eternal existence and love in His Word.

Hebrews 13:8 states, "Jesus Christ [is] the same yesterday and today, [yes] and forever."

In Psalm 102:27, we read, "But Thou art the same, and Thy years will not come to an end." And also, "But the lovingkindness of the LORD is from everlasting to everlasting on those who fear Him, and His righteousness to children's children" (103:17).

And again, in James 1:17, the Bible says, "Every good thing bestowed and every perfect gift is from above, coming down from the Father of lights, with whom there is no variation, or shifting shadow."

The world we live in and the circumstances around us change constantly.

Several years ago my husband and I went on quite a journey. We drove over six thousand miles from Palmdale, California, to Omaha, Nebraska, to Panama City, Florida, back up to Omaha, and then finally home to California! We were gone almost one month, had left our youngest daughter at home in Palmdale, settled our middle child in Omaha to begin medical school, and spent some time with our oldest son and his wife in Florida.

During that same period, we closed escrow on a home, found renters for a home we used to live in, had our van broken into in Nebraska, said some difficult goodbyes, and opened escrow on a new home.

The changing circumstances of our lives seemed to be reflected in the continually changing scenery along our drive: flat deserts, rolling hills, majestic mountains, and altitudes of just above sea level to over twelve thousand feet high. There were glaciers through the highest passes of the Rockies and marshlands through Alabama. Temperatures ranged from the low 60s to over 110 degrees.

Our lives, the people in them, and the circumstances surrounding us can change just as frequently as the variations we experienced on our drive across the country.

Health, families, friends, and physical possessions can all be gone or changed forever in an instant. When I was a young mom, I went from living in a large home with my three small children, two of them just toddlers, to living in a tiny apartment in government subsidized housing for the poor.

There is not even a guarantee that we'll be able to hold on to our mental capabilities or awareness. This is a bit unsettling, but it is the truth.

I first wrote this book to present as a retreat in 2006. Since that time, my husband has been diagnosed with early onset Alzheimer's/dementia. Perhaps God was preparing my heart for what was to come.

Change is real; sometimes it is beneficial, and sometimes it is difficult. I am extremely thankful for the constancy of my Lord and Savior and His care for me and those I love.

The words "to have and to hold" applied to human relationships are only as reliable as the people who profess them, and we often fail, either of our own accord or because of things beyond our control.

Do you follow through with everything you say?

Our intentions may be heartfelt, but our capacity to see things through is often weak. For example, I've told countless people that I care about them and I am sincere when sharing those sentiments with my family and friends. However, I can unfortunately report to you that I have either unwillingly or unknowingly hurt many of them in some way at some time. I have said things without thinking and then I do not remember the promises I've made.

Though my heart wants to be a picture of Jesus' love and I desire to be true to my promises and commitments, I can fail miserably even with the best intentions. This is discouraging, but it accurately sets the stage for what we can be sure of.

"To have and to hold from this day forward," when used in reference to Christ's relationship with us, is an absolute certainty and truly is a much more appropriate application than the vow made between two people. Unlike all the circumstances of our lives that can fluctuate, Jesus alone remains constant and sure. We can find complete security in Him.

God has us and He holds us forever.

This security affords us His protection and care. A child of God has continuous, unwavering, absolute, inviolable, perfect shelter in the palm of their Savior's hands. Read what Psalm 125:1–2 says below:

> Those who trust in the LORD are as Mount Zion, which cannot be moved, but abides forever. As the mountains surround Jerusalem, so the LORD surrounds His people from this time forth and forever.

Here's a quick geography lesson. The city of Jerusalem was naturally fortified almost completely surrounded with steep mountains and deep valleys. This natural landscape offered protection, and Jerusalem was considered highly impenetrable.

The Bible paints for us this wonderful picture of God encircling us just as the mountains and valleys shielded Jerusalem from attack. Although we may or may not be geographically surrounded by mountains and valleys like Jerusalem, God covers us with His mighty protection. He is our fortification, our defense, and our stronghold.

Psalm 91:4 says God will cover us with His pinions, "And under His wings you may seek refuge …" I love this illustration of God's possessive care.

I enjoy spending time outside. In the morning, when the weather is nice, which in California is most of the time, I can be found enjoying a cup of coffee outside with my husband. We like to take in the sights and sounds of the outdoors.

We are always excited to see the new baby birds. In the spring, it is fun to watch nests being built in nearby bushes and trees. Twice, a hummingbird built its nest in the crook of an outside light fixture. It was in a place where there was protection from the weather since it was covered. Except we had a cat. It was obvious that the mother birds didn't appreciate its presence. They would fearlessly zoom in on the cat and squawk loudly to defend a safe zone for their young babies. Rarely would the cat even get a chance to get close to the nest.

The watchful parents would continuously be on the lookout to fight off any signs of intrusion and put up a fuss at the slightest hint of danger. We weren't even able to walk near this light fixture, let alone turn it on, without the fear of getting dive-bombed! You could say the mother bird had claimed its domain, put her stamp on it, and forced us out of our own patio. I suppose we could have strong-armed her into leaving, but it was too sweet a picture to disrupt.

We have an amazing Father who has promised us His protection. He desires to keep us from harm, from falling out of the nest, if you will. He tells us in His Word that once we are His, no one will be able to snatch us away from Him. I referenced John 10:27 in chapter 1. I'll expand this reference here.

John 10:27–29 states, "My sheep hear My voice, and I know them, and they follow Me; and I give eternal life to them, and they shall never perish; and no one shall snatch them out of My hand. My Father, who has given [them] to Me, is greater than all; and no one is able to snatch [them] out of the Father's hand."

When we respond to Jesus and accept His promise, our entire focus is drawn upward as God prepares us for that day of glory when we will be in heaven with Him and presented as His bride. We can rest in the fact that we belong to God. He holds us in His hands forever. Colossians 3:1 speaks of that heavenward focus: "If then you have been raised up with Christ, keep seeking the things above, where Christ is, seated at the right hand of God."

We are God's possession. He will hold us, He will guard us, and He will sustain us. This is His promise to His children and it cannot be broken.

Following are the rewritten vows from chapters 1 and 2:

Until Death Do We Meet

(I take you): I confess You, Jesus Christ, are God. You became flesh, lived as man, and died for my sins.

(To be my lawfully wedded): I receive You as my Savior and Lord.

(To have and to hold from this day forward): I trust that no one will be able to snatch me out of Your hands and that I will be known as Yours forevermore.

CHAPTER 3

*For Better or
for Worse*

There are two goals I pray for in anything I write. The first is to encourage each of God's children to dig deeper into His truths, to recognize the incredible blessings we have in Jesus, and to live lives that are victorious in His strength. The second is to urge those who may desire to know more about God to seek movement toward a saving relationship with Him so that we might all rejoice together in His eternal presence.

I pray that you are challenged just as I am by pouring through His Word and being reminded of His great love for us and the strength that is available through His Holy Spirit.

In this book, I've taken traditional wedding vows that we've all heard and applied them to the church as a group of believers described as Christ's bride. Rewriting these vows to Jesus causes our focus to be drawn to our glorious union with Christ when He calls each of His children home.

Below is a short review and explanation of what has developed so far in our vows:

(I take you): I confess You, Jesus Christ, are God, that You became flesh, lived as man, and died for my sins.

(To be my): I receive You as my Savior and Lord. Once we've accepted God's proposal to us and have confessed Jesus as our Lord and Savior, we've entered into a covenant with Him. We then become heirs as God's beloved and are given the riches of heaven. Just as a citizen of another country has an opportunity to become a citizen of the United States through marriage, our citizenship changes from earth to heaven once we accept God's proposal of salvation through His Son, Jesus. Ephesians 2:19 says, "So then you are no longer strangers and aliens, but you are fellow citizens with the saints, and are of God's household."

(To have and to hold from this day forward): I hang on to Your promise that no one will be able to snatch me out of Your hands and that I will be known as Yours forevermore.

Now I'll set the stage for the next section of our vows, "for better or for worse."

Picture a group of teenagers at school. One day they are best of friends with someone and the next, they aren't speaking well of one another. Think of the families you are acquainted with. Perhaps those in your neighborhood, your own relatives, or even those you've been friends with for years. At one moment all seems to be going well in a family, then overnight chaos is reigning in relationships. It is the same in almost every situation you can imagine. People can be very inconsistent with their feelings toward one another. Unlike the constant changes we experience here on earth, our relationship with Christ is permanent. His love for us does not waver depending on what we did or didn't do, or what we said or didn't say. His promise of eternal life and His protection are secure.

As Christ's betrothed, we are looking forward to that day when He redeems us for His own. This causes our focus here on earth to change and be directed to that day of glory.

The next line in typical wedding vows reads, "For better or for worse."

When we look at the word *better*, our focus will be on the abundant blessings that become ours as God's beloved.

First, there's the gift of heaven itself, which is the promise of everlasting life with the one who has captured our hearts. We are heirs to a kingdom, and God is preparing a place for us right now even as we look at His Word together. This is an incredible truth to hold on to.

Several years ago in September, my mom and I spent a day on Catalina Island off the California coast. We enjoyed a tour of Avalon while a guide narrated the history of many of the landmark buildings. As we drove by a gorgeous home overlooking the bay, we listened to the sad history behind its construction.

The story goes like this. A young man just betrothed to his beloved began building her a beautiful dwelling that they would enjoy after their marriage. He worked on this home tirelessly, looking forward to the day he would finally bring his bride home. When the mansion was completed, he waited with great anticipation for her arrival for their wedding day. However, she didn't show up. Apparently she had changed her mind and never returned to the island.

The young man was so devastated, he forbid any female to enter the home he had built. For more than forty years, the structure was abandoned. It was kept up but not enjoyed, not lived in by its intended couple, and therefore not loved in either.

This is a tragic account, and although most of us do not have as graphic a story as this one to tell, we have all experienced broken promises from people we've loved, either in friendships, among family members, or even within a marriage. Words said or vows taken by people are often unreliable; God's promise of love to His children is absolute.

In the book of John, it says, "Let not your heart be troubled; believe in God, believe also in Me. In My Father's house are many dwelling places; if it were not so, I would have told you; for I go to prepare a place for you. And if I go and prepare a place for you, I will come again, and receive you to Myself; that where I am, [there] you may be also" (John 14:1–3).

It is certain that Jesus will return and His children will reside in heaven with Him. There is no doubt!

I remember vividly my son's first day of school. I lived with my three young children in an apartment at that time, and he was very excited to take the bus to kindergarten. The pickup and drop-off was located on the corner of the large complex, so we walked there together in the morning. The plan was for me to meet him back there in the afternoon when the bus dropped him off. I can still picture him in my mind's eye, wearing his backpack with his carefully packed lunch, acting all grown-up at five.

I completely lost track of time, and it was about fifteen minutes after he was scheduled to be dropped off at home when I realized I was late! You can probably feel my sense of panic! I hurried to the corner expecting to find him standing alone and probably crying. To my horror, he wasn't there at all! Failure at motherhood, right? I quickly called the school and tried to stay calm as they tracked down the bus driver on his radio.

I found out that the bus driver would not let my son off the bus with no one to meet him—praise God! I was reassured on the phone that my son was on the bus, sitting right up front, having a great time riding all over the valley in the school bus as the driver's right-hand man! I was supposed to have met him at noon; he finally arrived home at three.

He was very excited to tell me all about his fun adventure. I actually had to disappoint him and let him know that this was not going to happen each day after school. Needless to say, I was mortified at my ability to forget my own child, but God's grace covered both of us.

Jesus *will* be waiting for us. He anticipates our coming home, and there is no danger that He will forget to meet His children!

Earlier, I wrote about the blessing of God's protection in our lives and the assurance that is ours in Him. His love for us will never be thwarted. Unlike the ever-changing things of this earth, God, His character, and His promises remain the same. His love for us, His desire for us to be with Him, and His care for us are always constant and true to His perfect faithfulness.

God has not only given His children protection, but also the gift of His Holy Spirit. "The fruits of the Spirit" is a fairly common phrase used in Christian settings. They are listed in Galatians 5:22–23: love, joy, peace, patience, kindness, goodness, faithfulness, gentleness, and self-control. These words are a description of the qualities that are developed in an individual seeking after God and under the influence of His Spirit. Talk about blessings!

Without the Spirit working in our lives, it is impossible to love those who hate, to experience joy in the midst of sadness, to feel peace during turmoil, to be patient under trying circumstances, to act in kindness toward those who are seeking to destroy, to act in goodness when it seems that most everything surrounding us is bent on evil, to be faithful when others are unreliable, to be gentle when harshness is prevalent, and to practice self-control when restraint has become obsolete.

God knows we are incapable of acting in a manner that is pleasing to Him without His helper, the Holy Spirit. The blessing of the Holy Spirit in our lives enables us to live as lights in a world ruled by darkness. Think again about the qualities listed earlier. How contrary to the world is this kind of behavior?

In our own strength, we return dislike with aversion, we allow sadness to overtake happiness, we are unsettled when trouble is present, we lose our patience, we answer harshly toward those who are mean, we act according to the moment and circumstances around us, we distrust when others prove to be flakey, we use harsh words toward others, and self-control is almost nonexistent.

Phrases like "road rage" and groups of people rallying, holding up signs pitted against one another, are all too common. It is not unusual to hear of a violent crime committed simply because someone didn't like a person or circumstance or felt deserved of something that another possessed. Our natural tendency is to react out of preservation of self, no matter the cost or consequence to others.

How often do you remember to thank God for the blessing of His Spirit, which allows you to act in a manner of love toward others regardless of how you are treated?

Let's now turn our attention to the word *worse* in our vows. Think of the blessings listed earlier and ask yourself if you always use what's available to act in love. Unfortunately, I can assure you that there are many times I do not take hold of the power given to me to avoid sin. But once again, God knows us well enough to know we will fail, and He uses circumstances in our lives to teach us and continue to guide us toward acting in a way that is becoming to His character.

God is continually preparing us, through His loving discipline, to be presented to Him as a perfect bride without stain or wrinkle or any other blemish, but holy and blameless.

Ephesians 5:26–27 says that "He might sanctify her, having cleansed her by the washing of water with the word, that He might present to Himself the church in all her glory, having no spot or wrinkle or any such thing; but that she should be holy and blameless."

Most of us realize that there are negative consequences for poor choices. Certainly, we have all experienced the result of sinful decisions we've made. There's no blame to pin on anyone but ourselves when we are disciplined for bad behavior. We even accept, perhaps begrudgingly, that we get caught or have to pay the price for our actions that are contrary to God's commands.

Hopefully, we all learn from this and think a bit more carefully before repeating the same poor decisions. This kind of correction seems appropriate to almost everyone, and we know that God is faithful to forgive.

But what about when we have tried to pay attention to do what is right and we find ourselves under some kind of attack or difficulty? This happens to each of us at one time or another. You spend time asking God to search your heart and show you the sin that you have not noticed. Nothing seems to be glaringly wrong, and while this fact is encouraging, it can also leave you feeling confused and discouraged.

So often we view the word *discipline* as punishment for doing wrong. None of us enjoy punishment. I am unable to recall a time when any of my own children asked me to discipline them. Imagine hearing the words, "Mommy, please give me more correction."

On a humorous note, several times I have seen my young grandchildren put themselves in a time out. The first time I realized what was happening, I actually heard one of my three-year-old grandsons groan, begin to count out loud, and remove himself from the room. I'm not sure how their parents have accomplished this, but on more than one occasion, I've seen a grandchild walk to a designated corner or space, sit down, and begin counting out loud. Then I hear this voice saying, "Okay, Mommy, I'm calm now," or "I'm sorry, Mommy." And not just one of my grandchildren does this; several from different families do the same. I feel they have found some sort of magic key and need to share this valuable discipline technique with others!

When people have children, why do they teach or train them? Because they love them and want to instruct them to recognize right from wrong. Think of how you might teach a child not to run across a busy street. You would not allow a child to take a chance of being hit by a car for him or her to understand the dangers of that behavior. The hope is that through instruction, the child will avoid the consequences of choices that could lead to serious trouble.

Similar words that explain discipline are *teaching* and *training*. God trains us through adversity. He allows difficulties in our lives to teach us to lean on His strength and look to His righteousness.

Hebrews 12:7–11 paints a tender picture of God's commitment to discipline us as His beloved children. In fact, only those whom God loves are disciplined by Him for the purpose of teaching holiness. Hebrews 12:9 reads, "But if you are without discipline, of which all have become partakers, then you are illegitimate children and not sons." God's discipline in our lives actually assures us of our genuine relationship with Him.

Think of it this way. How would you regard a parent's commitment toward his or her children if the parent never taught them anything? Imagine a child being left alone to fend for themself. A genuine love for someone causes us to desire the best for them. We want to guide those we care about away from the things that will cause them either immediate or future difficulty.

Spiritual discipline in our lives produces godly character. By it we are trained to respond righteously in negative situations. The discipline God allows helps us to curb the passions that may easily become priorities over God. Unlike the times I've become tired and frustrated and wanted to give up when training my children,

God is always faithful to the task of teaching us His ways and He does it with perfect understanding.

I grew up in a family with four children. I can remember my mom sometimes being so exhausted that when there was a problem between the kids, we would all get punished simply because she didn't have the energy to sort all the facts.

I've done the same thing when my kids were young. You may be familiar with this scenario. "Mommmmmmmmy, he's looking at me!" Then you hear, "I am not!" "Mommmmmmy, she touched my leg" followed by "You touched me first!" Then "Stop making faces at me or I'll tell!" followed by "If you tell on me, I'll tell Mom what you did!" On and on it goes. Visualize the picture. It's about this time when you have heard enough and collectively bring down the gauntlet on all. Everyone is sent to their rooms for a time out. You are not really even interested in the facts; you just want peace and quiet for a moment. This may not be the best parenting scenario, but most readers will be able to relate!

Well, again, unlike us, God disciplines with a perfect love, perfect instruction, and perfect correction, and He never gives up or gets tired! He does not need to sort out the facts because He knows exactly where we err, and He is always perfectly just in His punishment.

Most individuals have gone through difficult times. It is often easier to have someone by your side when hardship comes knocking on your door. There is an ability to stand stronger when you feel supported by those who are watching out for your best interests.

When we go through trials, Jesus is right by our side. He does not run when it gets tough, and He knows better than we do what we need each moment to survive.

Psalm 46:1–3 tells us, "God is our refuge and strength, a very present help in trouble. Therefore we will not fear, though the earth should change, and though the mountains slip into the heart of the sea; though its waters roar [and] foam, though the mountains quake at its swelling pride."

We've looked at the "for better" statement in our vows, which are the abundant blessings we have in Christ. The blessings that are poured upon us are so numerous that we truly cannot begin to count them nor are we even aware of all of them. Take a moment to think of the air you breathe and the food you eat. If you are able to walk and talk, that is a blessing! A place of employment is a blessing. You could go on and on with listing blessings that come from God simply because He loves His children. I am a visual person, so I appreciate the color and texture of what is around me. Beautiful fall colors and the bright green of new grass are pleasing to my eyes.

Not only are the pleasant things or the "better" things blessings, but also the "worse" things as they are evidence of our salvation and the discipline and training we receive from God. He cares about you enough to guide and teach you in His ways. The "for worse" declaration in our vows can be viewed as the consequences God allows to correct sin and the discipline God uses to train us in righteousness. We'll take a closer look at more specific trials when we look at the words *poorer* and *sickness*.

God is in it for the long run. He will not quit working on His children. God will not check out when it gets hard. He is faithful to complete His work in us. He will see it through until each is home with Him for eternity.

1 Corinthians 1:9 tells us, "God is faithful, and through whom you were called into fellowship with His Son, Jesus Christ our Lord."

How about you? Are you in it for the long haul? When it gets tough, do you have a plan that will keep you close to His strength and endurance? Are you holding His hand through this journey when it's enjoyable *and* when it's difficult?

"I confess You, Jesus Christ, are God, that You became flesh, lived as man, and died for my sins. I receive You as my Savior and Lord. I know that no one will be able to snatch me out of Your hands. I will be known as Yours forevermore. As Your child, You promise me abundant blessings. Because I belong to You, I can expect Your loving discipline in my life to encourage me, to correct me, and to grow me."

CHAPTER 4

For Richer, for Poorer

For Richer ...

Typically, when we think of being rich, we think of financial resources. In a wedding ceremony, when these words are recited, the full impact of being rich or poor literally is seldom understood by everyone to its real extent.

Most of us have many resources readily available to us. Much more than the necessities of food and shelter. When a couple is in the throes of planning a wedding and even when they are in front of the attendant leading their vows, they are usually so in love that vowing their commitment to each other in times of prosperity and poverty is a no-brainer. You've heard the words "love will keep us together." These words are popular and were first recorded and released as a song by Neil Sedaka in 1973.

What does it mean to be rich? Having riches is so much more than owning tangible items. It is having an abundance of something. We can have an abundance of friends. We can be rich in information or have had a rich experience. Some individuals are rich in their abilities.

All individuals are rich in the blessings that God has showered upon His creation. Even those who have not accepted His gift of salvation reap benefits of His blessings.

In the last half of Matthew 5:45, it says, "For He causes His sun to rise on [the] evil and [the] good, and sends rain on [the] righteous and [the] unrighteous." All creation has an abundance of blessings given them by God. Just look around you. Focus on what is right and positive and beautiful, and you will find many riches from God's hand in the world.

It seems as if remaining faithful to our vows and commitments in times of prosperity and riches would be easy. Of course you would stick with someone when all is well and there is only enjoyment to be had, right? Let's pursue that thought.

We have all been through hills and valleys, times we would view as the good and the bad. Think of those periods of abundance and prosperity, when things are going well and life is comfortable. Aren't we sometimes more vulnerable to losing our focus than when things are a bit tough? It's very possible to forget our need for Christ in the better times, when we have abundance, when things are going well. Sure, we know He's there and that He will be ever faithful to rescue us when necessary, but we can develop a confidence in ourselves and our own abilities, forgetting the one who provided them. It's like thinking, *I'm doing okay right now, God; I'll catch you later.*

Consider for a moment just one of God's blessings, a blessing most of us take for granted. Most of us are able to think. We have a magnificent ability to understand information and concepts.

I'm always amazed at the creativity and the ways people's minds work. People are smart, they're intelligent, and their capacity for knowledge seems to be without bounds.

Each of us is uniquely different. Technology has advanced to degrees way beyond my comprehension. And it is all because of God. He has provided humankind with brains that are creative and inventive. These very blessings can sometimes cause us to think so highly of ourselves that we forget our need and forge ahead on our own. In fact, our success can easily become our focus (and our failure).

Some value their own thinking so highly that they have convinced themselves what is and is not necessary in their own spiritual connections with God. I recently had a conversation with a very intelligent and well-versed man who had studied various religions and devised the conclusion that his was a personal relationship with God based upon what he had chosen to believe. In essence, this man had decided to follow himself and happily went on his way. He had elevated his own intelligence—the intelligence God gave him—above the Savior of the world. Sad. Tragic.

Do you know individuals whose jobs, positions, titles, responsibilities, or successes have in any way become the center of their lives, actually defining their purpose and person?

Maybe you do not see your strength in the corporate sector, so there is no chance of your position or title overtaking your focus. "Hello, my name is Mom" does not hold much weight in a society built upon education and learned intelligence. Even the title of domestic engineer, although smiled at, does not ring bells in the ears of the hearer. But if you are in that category, you are not off the hook here. You can allow your schedule or responsibilities to become your focus no matter where you've been placed.

Perhaps you are an incredible organizer at home and have visions of yourself being a supermom. Then your pursuit can be an intense need to schedule everything with the necessity to see completion of all tasks on your list for the day.

The point is, when things are rich and there seem to be no troubles, you can become unfaithful to God as other things become more important. To get carried away by the blessings you've been given seems a bit ironic, but it happens all the time.

If you have recognized the need for a Savior to keep you from eternal damnation and have accepted the fact that the King of the universe knew your bleak future and chose to die for you, then how could you believe even for an instant that you are okay on your own?

I confess there are times when I go there and do not even realize it. Perhaps you can relate. We can get in this mode where we think we can do it all.

A few of you may be able to remember a television show that aired years ago called *Leave It to Beaver.* Let me introduce two of the characters. June Cleaver was the mother's name and her youngest son, Theodore, was nicknamed Beaver. This show was popular in the '60s and '70s and played during prime time in black and white!

I'll digress a bit here and indulge in the memory of going to the local drug store with my dad—for us it was the corner Thrifty's—with a box of blown-out tubes from the back of the television.

At the store, you would plug the used tubes into a tester to see which ones needed to be replaced. This was actually a fun thing to do, kind of like playing a game. You would sort through the burned out tubes and find the matching ones with the same number. They all came in their individual paper boxes. Then, when you got home, these new tubes would be placed into the back of the television, like a puzzle. The back of the unit would be replaced, you would plug it in, and then, if everything was done correctly, you could watch the television, or "tube" as it became known!

Of course, this was only if you were lucky enough to be able to adjust the rabbit ears sitting on top of the box so that most of the snow in the picture was eliminated. Some are smiling at this memory, and some are completely lost.

Back to our television character, June Cleaver. She was the perfect picture of a dutiful wife—always in a crisply ironed cotton dress with a lace collar and an apron with a bow in the back tied just so, a feather duster in one hand and, of course, practical high-heeled pumps!

She looked completely put together at all times, and she also never uttered a cross word. All meals were prepared and presented beautifully right on time. For snacks, freshly baked cookies were placed on a pretty ceramic plate at the ready for her family along with a glass of cold milk.

Somehow, she still had time to volunteer, sit with her husband, and counsel her children. She would never, ever be caught running to the grocery store without makeup. Wearing sweats, other than for exercising, and dropping her children off at school while wearing slippers in the car would never have crossed her mind.

Of course, our more modern-day picture might look a bit different. Perhaps the attire would be cute leggings and a top in size extra small with a dumbbell in one hand and the latest style of running shoes and the all-important no-show socks! Her long, shiny hair would be pulled back in a stylish ponytail and a basket of organic snacks would be on the counter with zero-calorie vitamin water lined up in the fridge.

Our modern-day picture of the perfect wife would still have time to volunteer, hold down a full-time career, care for her husband, and plan her children's schedules to perfection so each was adequately involved in outside activities. As a side note, her dog would always sit when told and would never, ever relieve itself on the kitchen floor! This woman would also closely monitor her five-year-old's college preparatory work in order that all Ivy League schools would vie over the child's acceptance in the future.

Well, when my family was young, I might have sometimes fooled myself into thinking I could do it all, but then I was quickly reminded how weak I was. Dinner was not always ready and was not always healthy. My kids' clothing didn't always match and yes, sometimes the cleanliness of a T-shirt could have been questioned.

Oh and my children weren't angels. The dog and cat were also not exemplary in their actions. I am guilty of wearing slippers in the car, I've uttered words that do not sound polite, and on and on it goes. But these memories become dim, and when things are going well, I can divert my focus. I allow myself to think I have it all under control instead of remembering that God is the one who holds everything together.

For example, when I originally wrote this some of the material in this book for a retreat, I began working on it quite a few months before I was scheduled to present it. My head said no problem because I love to write and speak. Writing and studying God's Word and sharing His truths with a group of people is my happy place. The outline was put into place months beforehand and the subject was broken down into sessions. I had my list of Bible verses, cross-references, and definitions. I spent hours praying, reading, writing, rewriting, and double-checking references.

This process was not new to me, and I understood that it would be enveloped in waiting—waiting on God for His words, spoken to my heart, and being reminded that this was His work, not mine.

So as much as I can report to you that I understand how this process works, I can also relate to you that I need to remind myself again and again to rely upon His help, His strength, and His direction instead of on myself. Head knowledge does nothing for us if it does not move to a heart change resulting in action. I can go into automatic mode. I am task oriented. When things are going well, in the better times, I can begin to function independently of everyone and everything else, including God. This is not acceptable.

I was scheduled to speak in Texas one month before I shared the same information in California. Two weeks before I was to leave, I still didn't have all the material in one nice cohesive package. It just wasn't pulling together.

As I began to realize my deadline was closing in, my husband mentioned that perhaps I should cancel some appointments the following week. This would lighten my schedule and provide the time to complete everything well, to do some rewriting, and add some final changes if needed. My response to his advice? "I'm doing fine; I can do it. Everything's under control."

Argh! Listen to those words! How many times do we say, "I'm doing just fine"? Do you know what that means? Read this definition of *fine*: being in a satisfactory condition. Meaning I'm all right, okay, or doing very well. This was not a justified answer on my part. I wasn't okay, and the reality was I was beginning to feel a bit overwhelmed. But I was intent on relying upon my own strength and the picture of having it all together.

By God's grace and the conviction of His Holy Spirit, I did end up taking my husband's advice. I cancelled some commitments and was blessed with a period of concentrated time to finish things well. Praise God for using people in our lives to keep us focused.

Our thoughts, direction, and purpose can change so quickly, especially when things are going well, that we can find ourselves on a different path without even realizing we turned away. Our commitment to God can take a U-turn in the better times! Thankfully, God's commitment to His children never wanes, even when we forget to acknowledge Him.

We need to be careful to continue to keep our focus on our need for God during the blessing of richer times. God knows this is an area where we will stumble, so He graciously gives us written instruction in His Word.

I recently had a conversation with someone who had helped me to remain focused on God while I was a young single mom. This person was a committed believer in Jesus and was definitely encouraging to me. After several years of no contact, I heard of the financial success of this person. After speaking with the person and even checking into the person's pursuits, I realized there was no clear mention of God in statements of the person's business. My heart reeled with disappointment at how this could have happened. Initially, God was the focus and source, but unfortunately, success became a distraction.

In Deuteronomy 28:1–14, the nation of Israel is promised blessings if they are careful to follow God. Then in verse 15 all the way to verse 57, there is a list of curses sent by God to discipline the nation of Israel if they push God aside and forget to live in dependence upon Him. In the first part of Isaiah 17:10, speaking again to the nation of Israel, God says, "For you have forgotten the God of your salvation and have not remembered the rock of your refuge."

Ouch!

It's seems obvious that we would heartily receive God's blessings—the richer times. But sometimes we can become engrossed in the enjoyment of having fun and wonderful experiences and push away the one who planned and made available those times in our lives.

We all have choices to make. In those times of blessings, when things in our lives seem to be going well, we can be especially vulnerable to forgetting God. God is the one who has bestowed blessings upon us. May He give us the grace to purposefully serve Him with all our hearts, souls, and minds *at all times*, focused on the true treasure of eternal life.

In periods of prosperity, whether it be riches or simply a time void of problems, we need to be careful that we do not divert our eyes elsewhere even for a moment. Without God, we are not okay.

We have been promised the riches of heaven and His everlasting and perfect care of our souls. This is not a gift we can receive without having a sincere reaction to observe His statutes, to live for Him, and to acknowledge His goodness in all things.

We experience the riches of having a relationship with God as His children if we have been saved by His grace. Everything needed to prosper in this world for His glory is afforded to us through Him.

For Poorer

2 Corinthians 1:5 says, "For just as the sufferings of Christ are ours in abundance, so also our comfort is abundant through Christ."

Okay, perhaps you have no issues accepting Jesus as your Lord and Savior in times of riches. In fact, you might say, "Bring it on!" But what about those times of hardship, the poorer times?

Traditional wedding vows say we will remain faithful even in the poorer times. These vows probably refer specifically to poor being the lack of finances. Most of us are clueless to how poor things can get. When you are newly married, it's difficult to imagine anything beyond the blissful feelings you have. Nothing would be able to thwart that, right? It's the storybook idea of just being together, even without a dime. We are convinced it's all that's needed to be happy and remain faithful.

Think back to when you were first saved, when God miraculously touched your heart and opened your eyes to understand His truths. It's phenomenal, right? The peace that ensues once you realize you do not have to have everything under control and you can lean on God's strength and trust in His perfect faithfulness is incredible.

When a heart of faith is born, there truly is no describing the change. If you've accepted the gospel, meaning you've been saved by grace through faith alone, then you can absolutely relate to the above. However, along with immediate peace and the beginnings of a transformed life, we are also promised hardship—the poor times.

Read 2 Timothy 3:12: "And indeed, all who desire to live godly in Christ Jesus will be persecuted." The word *persecuted* here means to suffer.

Psalm 34:19 also speaks of difficulties. It says, "Many are the afflictions of the righteous; but the LORD delivers him out of them all." Did you read that? It says many are the afflictions! We will encounter adversity, calamity, distress, misery, and trouble as we follow God.

In Matthew 16:24, Jesus told His disciples, "If anyone wishes to come after Me, let him deny [disown, abstain] himself, and take up his cross, and follow Me." To deny ourselves means it's not about us! We are to abstain from thinking upon our own desires and even needs in order to follow Christ. This means we may be exposed to suffering.

God cares for us and knows when things are especially tough. It seems a very long time ago that my three young children and I moved from place to place—roughly every six months for a period of three years. I had certainly not planned on being a single mom, and the relocations were not by choice but necessity. We were trying to survive in what felt like a harsh world at that time.

Financially, we were labeled as poor. We received government assistance for breakfasts and lunches at school and qualified for housing in a subsidized apartment project. I was the young mom standing in line in the government services office, a smile on my face, pretending I was okay even though inside my heart was crushed.

Just the remembrance of this time causes me to feel uneasy and close to tears. I can feel my heart racing and my stomach churning. I'm unable to describe how difficult it was to have to depend on government help to survive. I felt like a loser, and I certainly didn't want to be looked upon as a person who was unable to fend for herself. This is not an experience most of us would choose purposefully.

In those times, when circumstances seem especially bleak, we can draw closer to God and rely on all the resources we have in Him as His children, or we can allow ourselves to be distanced and grow apart from Him by adopting a woe-is-me attitude.

We may want to think that perhaps God has forgotten us, or even worse, that maybe there is not a God after all. The poorer times can be very difficult.

Perhaps you have never experienced financial poverty, praise God! But you can also feel poor in relationships, care, or love.

To be poor means to be without or not have sufficient means. And yet, even considering the poorest of poor, in Christ we do have everything, and we are never truly alone. We may not see abundance in possessions, we may even feel that no one cares or understands, but that is a lie. God always cares, and we have been given His eternal promises at the great cost of Jesus's suffering and death.

The riches of this life, God's mercies, are seldom complained about, but do grumblings surface when the difficulties appear? Do we remain faithful or do we go our own way, thinking we can do better on our own?

Those very vows that we eagerly recite as newlyweds are forgotten when circumstances are trying. We all know of marriages that cease to exist because one or both parties have decided it's not as much fun as they thought it would be. Faithfulness to the vow of staying together in the poor times has almost become obsolete.

Pause and remember for a moment the story of Job. He lost almost everything, and when his wife suggested that he turn from

God, he responded with this statement: "You speak as one of the foolish women speaks. Shall we indeed accept good from God and not accept adversity?" In all this, Job did not sin with his lips (Job 2:10).

In an earlier chapter, I made a parallel between God's protection over us and a mother bird covering her young with her outstretched wings. In Matthew 6:26, we read another description of God's care for us: "Look at the birds of the air, that they do not sow, neither do they reap, nor gather into barns, and [yet] your heavenly Father feeds them. Are you not worth much more than they?"

The times of need in our lives remind us to look to God as our provider. He is the source of everything we require. Often, the more difficult times are necessary in order to grow our determination to follow God.

Following is a lengthy section of scripture that beautifully describes God's promises to His children and our response toward Him:

> Grace and peace be multiplied to you in the knowledge of God and of Jesus our Lord; seeing that His divine power has granted to us everything pertaining to life and godliness, through the true knowledge of Him who called us by His own glory and excellence. For by these He has granted to us His precious and magnificent promises, in order that by them you might become partakers of [the] divine nature, having escaped the corruption that is in the world by lust. Now for this very reason also, applying all diligence, in your faith supply moral excellence, and in [your] moral excellence, knowledge; and in [your] knowledge, self-control, and in [your] self-control, perseverance, and in [your] perseverance, godliness; and in [your]

godliness, brotherly kindness, and in [your] brotherly kindness, love. For if these [qualities] are yours and are increasing, they render you neither useless nor unfruitful in the true knowledge of our Lord Jesus Christ. For he who lacks these [qualities] is blind [or] short-sighted, having forgotten [his] purification from his former sins. Therefore, brethren, be all the more diligent to make certain about His calling and choosing you; for as long as you practice these things, you will never stumble. (2 Peter 1:2–10)

The apostle Paul tells us to focus on God, not on circumstances here on earth (Colossians 3:2). We know the difficult times will come. The times when we feel poor in possessions, relationships, circumstances, or health.

Suffering for what you love builds a steadfast commitment to continue through whatever may come. God is aware of our struggles, and He tells us to stay focused on Him.

Remember, Christ carried a cross in obedience to His Father.

In Colossians 3:2, the word *set* means to be intent on. Our minds, our affection, and our mental disposition need to be earnestly looking in a certain direction toward God. This means we develop an intensive interest to savor and to keep thinking about our Savior.

Do you go to God with an appreciation and intent to delight in His truths? In a busy world, the art of unhurried enjoyment and gratitude is rare.

We are to love heavenly things! We are to study them and let our hearts be entirely engrossed by the things of God.

Our minds—for better or for worse, for richer or for poorer—should be occupied with heaven and that day of glory when we are to be with Christ. Our feet may be on the earth, but our heads should be in the heavens!

When we accept God's proposal to us and receive Christ as our Savior, we are showered with blessings, trained by discipline, and through the help of the Holy Spirit, enabled to rejoice in times of plenty and in times of need.

The summary of our vows reads as follows:

Until Death Do We Meet

(I take you): I confess You, Jesus Christ, are God, that You became flesh, lived as man, and died for my sins.

(To be my): I receive You as my Savior and Lord.

(To have and to hold from this day forward): I know that no one will be able to snatch me out of Your hands and that I will be known as Yours forevermore.

(For better or for worse): As Your child, I am a recipient of Your abundant blessings, but I am also to expect discipline from You as my heavenly Father.

(For richer): I will rejoice in times of prosperity and blessing while keeping my focus and purpose on the one true treasure, which is eternal life.

(For poorer): I will also choose to rejoice in times of need and will look to You for all things, remembering You are the source of all blessings and all I could ever want is found in You.

We'll explore what it means to remain faithful "in sickness and in health" in the next chapter.

CHAPTER 5

In Sickness and in Health

We are abundantly blessed by God! Even the difficult times in our lives are used by Him for our benefit and for His glory. When things are going well, we need to be sure to remain focused instead of relying upon ourselves. When we are in need, we can still rejoice knowing God will provide all that is necessary.

God is always faithful in His relationship with us. He has saved us from the penalty of sin; He daily saves us from the control of sin if we are obedient; and He has promised His unwavering love and strength into eternity.

But do we remain faithful to His commands at all times, for better, for worse, in sickness and in health? God's faithfulness to us is a promise that cannot be broken. What does our faithfulness to God look like?

In Sickness

The experience of physical illness is a familiar subject to all of us. Chronic problems and serious diseases or the latest strain of flu virus and even seasonal allergies have plagued most of us or those we know at one time or another.

Our bodies, although amazingly created, are under sin's curse and deteriorate over time. As I celebrate each birthday, I notice that I do not move as quickly and I do not think as fast. As I look back only a decade ago, I can tell you emphatically that my body has changed, not so much in structure and shape, but in physical strength and endurance.

It used to be my muscles would hurt after some great physical exertion like a long hike or an intensive housecleaning or gardening day. Now, when I get out of bed in the morning, sometimes I notice my muscles ache! Go figure.

Some readers may be suffering from devastating illnesses, and I'm in no way making light of the load you are bearing. But the truth is we are all dying. Our physical bodies are in a process of decay. It is not as apparent when we are young because it does not begin to show up on the outside until we are somewhere in our forties or fifties. This is a magic time of life—things begin to disappear! Like the natural color in your hair and your close-up vision. Some things also seem to be sliding downhill. Have you noticed your cheeks and chin aren't where they used to be? The exciting news is, I'm finally thinning out—in my hair and eyebrows! If you're unable to relate to this, you have something to look forward to.

I remember when I turned fifty. I didn't feel any different, but my doctor gave me his personal birthday greetings in the form of a postcard—it was the gift of a free colonoscopy. I also received a full jug of a very special drink that I was to enjoy before this test. Thank you very much.

Think back to a time in your twenties, if you're able. Everyone around you seemed so much older, right? Perhaps not wiser, but older. I know I didn't have the right appreciation for age and wisdom when I was young, unfortunately.

Thirty seemed quite old, and I couldn't imagine being there. Then when thirty happened, forty seemed old, and I felt I'd never be able to relate to that age. The first time I used this material for a retreat, I was in my late forties, and recently I turned sixty! Time stands still for no one—except God.

While we are on this age progression, we'll take it a bit further. It seems that when you're in your eighties and beyond, people do not look at you as though you're old any longer. Suddenly, you become cute! My sweet mom just turned ninety-two, and she can get away with anything because she's cute. She even looks cute. Her wrinkles have found their resting place, and her snowy white hair rings her face.

Unfortunately, age seems to go hand in hand with increased illness. When we aren't feeling well, it's difficult to press forward. Our focus is affected, and we struggle to enjoy the fruits of the Spirit. Patience and kindness in particular can become distant ideas when I'm not feeling well. I have to pray through those times to continue to be an effective witness to those around me.

The trials of sickness that we endure is no surprise to God. He's given us some instruction for those times. 2 Corinthians 4:16 says, "Therefore we do not lose heart, but though our outer man is decaying, yet our inner man is being renewed day by day."

The word *decay* is translated as perish, meaning to rot thoroughly. I realize this is a horrible thought as you consider even the idea of rotting away.

We are all guilty of forgetting that piece of fruit in the bottom of a basket or the vegetables that have been left too long in the crisper drawer of the refrigerator. When you find these items, they have already begun to break down. Things decay, they decompose after a time. Not just fruit or vegetables, but lumber rots also.

Depending on where you live, termites help to break down old, rotting lumber. Years ago, I remember working in my in-laws garage after they had both passed away. I'm not sure anyone had even been in the garage for several years. Fortunately, it was a detached building, so it stood alone toward the back of a long driveway.

As my husband and I were trying to go through items that had been packed away for years, I heard a fairly loud crunching noise over and over again. Upon opening the drawer of an old antique dresser, I noticed it was very full of sawdust and the wood had rotted in places. Nests of termites had made their homes in the decaying wood! It still gives me the heebie-jeebies!

If you can get past the rotting element in 2 Corinthians, you will see there is encouragement in the verse also. We read that our "inner man" is being renewed.

Several times as I've passed by a mirror, I've been a bit startled to see an older-looking woman in the reflection. I just do not feel aged in my thinking and in my heart. In my soul, I'm still young! And, in fact, according the verse above, I'm being renovated inside. Maybe that's why my muscles feel sore in the morning. There is work going on!

I love finding old pieces of furniture to restore. Sanding off all the layers of stain, varnish, and paint yields the beautiful, original product. I like to think that's what's happening inside me. God, is sanding (okay, sometimes chipping or even hammering) away my sin. He is working on that new look I need for heaven! I am being renewed. What a pleasant thought.

Our bodies become weak through affliction, and we may not be as strong physically as we used to be, but we have a promise as believers that our minds and spirits are being renewed in strength daily. As this process happens, we are to not lose heart.

We are not to become weary as we witness our outer bodies getting old and falling apart. No time for sadness and mourning. It just means we are one step closer to heaven. We have something to look forward to. Focusing on what lies ahead instead of thinking upon what we are leaving behind will give us a heavenward view. We are being prepared for our future. We are here now for a purpose, and that purpose is to serve as we await our true home.

Consider the physical problems each of us deal with; for some, the list is long and the suffering hard. This can either become our focus and a description of who we are, or it can become just a part of our lives here on earth. In other words, I can think of myself as a person with (fill in the blank with all ailments, illnesses, aches, pains, and diseases), making it my identity, or I can think of myself as God's child, who happens to have physical issues that need attention sometimes. This thinking changes my focus to what is truly important and to the task at hand—being God's child with a mission to serve and to share truth.

I have a friend who has suffered cancer twice now, has lost a child, and has had more than her share of disappointments and heartache. Yet even going through her last bout of chemo, along with losing her hair once again, she smiles! And it's not fake, it's real. And she continues to serve in whatever way she is able, not allowing cancer to define who she is. Her inside joy comes from the knowledge that she is God's child. She truly is an example of keeping her focus heavenward!

2 Peter 3:8 says, "But do not let this one [fact] escape your notice, beloved, that with the Lord one day is as a thousand years, and a thousand years as one day."

Relatively speaking, time here is short. When we look at our time here on earth, it may seem our afflictions last for extended periods, but if we look at time in the context of eternity, the things we experience are mere moments. Think of a water glass that is half full. Now, pour out the water and set it aside. Remove the bottom from the glass and pour the water back in. What happens? It just flows without filling up. The familiar idiom of a glass being half full or half empty is an illustration of how we view circumstances. Time is relative to how we think also.

God's perspective of time reminds us where our focus should be—on eternity. Everything will one day be made new again (Revelation 21:1–6). What a contrast heaven will be to the life on earth we now know.

All things here are in a process of decay, including our earthly bodies. One day, we will exchange the corruptible for the incorruptible, the ragged for the renewed.

John 3:16 is a familiar verse to many of us: "For God so loved the world, that He gave His only begotten Son, that whoever believes in Him should not perish, but have eternal life." And in John 6:47, we read, "Truly, truly, I say to you, he who believes has eternal life." It is clear that eternal life is promised to the one who believes, and this promise is secure. It's not a maybe or an "I hope so."

John 10:28 also reiterates the truth that we can absolutely expect an eternal future: "And I give eternal life to them, and they shall never perish; and no one shall snatch them out of My hand."

Recall the story of Mary and Martha's brother Lazarus in John 11. Jesus loved this family, and when he heard that Lazarus was sick, He chose to travel there. Jesus knew Lazarus had already died, and by the time He arrived, Lazarus had been in the tomb four days. Martha went out to meet Jesus, and He encouraged her with the truths she knew and understood—that there was life eternal in Him. In John 11:25–26, we read Jesus's words, "I am the resurrection and the life; he who believes in Me shall live even if he dies, and everyone who lives and believes in Me shall never die. Do you believe this?"

The account of Lazarus's death and Jesus raising him from the dead is a story of incredible faith on the part of Mary and Martha, and also Jesus's love for those who trust in Him. I would encourage you to take a moment to read the full account of this interaction.

Upon contemplating periods of sickness or weakness in our lives, remembering the benefit of these times and the eternal outcome is an encouragement. Romans 6:22–23 gives us words to ponder: "But now having been freed from sin and enslaved to God, you derive your benefit, resulting in sanctification, and the outcome, eternal life. For the wages of sin is death, but the free gift of God is eternal life in Christ Jesus our Lord."

I definitely cannot comprehend all there is about eternity and what having an immortal spirit will be like. But I do know that in faith, I believe in Jesus's death and resurrection, that He is returning for His children, and that we will live forever with Him in a place bereft of sin and pain.

There is a passage in 1 Corinthians 15:12–55 that covers more of the idea of the perishable and imperishable that you may want to read for yourself.

Let's continue on with the necessity of remaining faithful through sickness and in health and the difficulties represented in both situations. I was married to my husband in 1991. Within the first three years of our marriage, we experienced the death of my husband's dad, my mother-in-law moving in with us, her death, a move, two surgeries, and the diagnosis of my husband's multiple sclerosis.

Daily struggles are associated with this disease. A plethora of injections, oral medications, monthly intravenous medications, home health visits, hospitalizations, tests, and office visits were routine. (On a side note, as my husband has gotten older, the MS has taken a bit of a hiatus, and we are thankful!)

Throughout our married life, there have been times where the focus has momentarily needed to be on treatments, but these physical sicknesses have never defined who my husband is. He had the choice of becoming overwhelmed by discouragement when he was unable to be the strength in our family that he wanted to be. He could have chosen to become disgruntled and disenchanted toward God. After all, we didn't start our marriage with illness, and it wasn't what we had planned.

But because of God's grace, I have been blessed with a great model of proven faith in my husband. He has always just kept moving forward, albeit sometimes with a cane, and his focus has remained fixed on God. He has taught me by example to do the same. Even now, as the clarity and quickness of my husband's thinking is challenged, he is gracefully accepting God's perfect plan.

So where is the blessing in sickness? Many of you know the answer from experience. You learn the only way to *not* lose your focus is by holding on to God's strength and guidance even when it gets tough and scary. You recognize with much more clarity your need for God and your absolute dependence on Him.

Paul experienced a thorn in his side, which seemed to be some kind of bodily annoyance or weakness, a frailty of some sort. The purpose of this discomfort is explained in 2 Corinthians 12:7. As Paul entreats the Lord to remove the problem, the answer he received was to depend on God's sufficiency.

2 Corinthians 12:9 states, "And He has said to me, 'My grace is sufficient for you, for power is perfected in weakness. Most gladly, therefore, I will rather boast about my weaknesses, that the power of Christ may dwell in me.'"

Sadly, most of us know individuals who have turned from God out of anger when devastating illness presented itself. Confusion, sadness, and a need to be in control all contribute to a decision to turn from the very One who provides comfort.

We can also turn away from people and our church family. Rarely, does everyone say the right thing. Others are seldom able to completely understand our woes. We can allow ourselves to become offended, thinking that others do not care if we are suffering. Or we can be stoic and decide to look like we can handle sickness on our own, not wanting to bother anyone. This neither serves nor allows people the opportunity to serve. The type of response above is not from a heart relying upon God in all things.

We have a choice. We can opt out and run, or we can trust. Perseverance and dependence on God in times of sickness and weakness honors Him.

And in Health

I often get to watch my young grandchildren. As they play, they are the picture of health and energy. Thankfully, most of us also enjoy seasons when we are healthy and energetic. How do we honor God in times of good health? Does it then become more about us because our immediate need is lessened? It is important to address this question.

In chapter 2, I wrote about how easy it is for us to push God aside when things are going well, or in the better times. We can also inadvertently trust in our own physical abilities when we feel well, when we are blessed with the picture of health and vigor. Consider how unstoppable you felt when you were in your twenties (if you're there now, rejoice and make the most of your youth). It's likely that your thinking was something comparable to *I can do anything!*

In those times when we feel strong and capable, remembering that God is the one who blessed us with time, energy, and abilities will help us to use everything we have for His glory.

Regardless if we are in a time of sickness or health, we are to serve hard in whatever capacity we are able. We are to serve when it's easy and when it's not so easy. Even when it requires extreme physical or mental effort and sacrifice.

Serving God through serving one another can be laborious, difficult, thankless, and physically and emotionally exhaustive. It often means we do not get to do what we think we might rather do. Sleep may be deprived and resources of all kinds may feel like they are being drained. Serving, however, is necessary to our relationship with God. It is an act of obedience. In serving others, we serve Him.

Romans 12:1 says, "I urge you therefore, brethren, by the mercies of God, to present your bodies a living and holy sacrifice, acceptable to God, [which is] your spiritual service of worship." Jesus came to serve—to die on a cross for us.

As my husband and I get a bit older and his medical issues increase, our serving does look different than it did perhaps ten or fifteen years ago. He no longer leads a weekly Bible study group and the preparation to teach Sunday school regularly has become almost impossible. But with God's strength and in His grace, he still serves. It is fun to watch as God continues to provide unique ways for my husband to serve. We both are excited for these opportunities.

So rather than slow down dramatically, I sometimes feel as if we are busier than ever, trying to make the most of what God has placed in our lives. Is it possible to serve too much? Well, think of how well you sleep when you're exhausted!

If God continues to enable you to serve, then you need to continue to do so whenever you're able. Typically I have a rather large list of things to get done. Recently, I was looking forward to a day with no commitments so I could apply myself to this list. Then I received a text asking us if we would be able to watch one of our grandchildren so that my daughter could fill in for someone who had called in sick at work.

Of course, the answer was yes. My husband had a tutoring appointment online, so I decided to take my four-year-old grandson to the mall. It was rainy and cold outside, so I figured we could walk around inside and look at the Christmas decorations in the stores. We had a wonderful time holding hands, taking silly pictures, and eating a lollipop!

My daughter was so appreciative because she knows how busy I am. We had a great conversation about using the time and energy we have today and considering priorities. My grandson does not care about my to-do list; he cares about spending time with me! The investment in memories and serving others has value way beyond our comprehension. And I like to think that my children will remember by my example what's truly important when they have opportunities to serve their grown children years from now.

There is no guarantee that you or I will be able to serve Him in the same capacity tomorrow or even at all, so as long as we have breath let's try to make wise use of our time and energy and pray that God will use us for His purposes here on earth. Our rest will be when we get home to the one who awaits us in heaven. Lord, help us to remember why we are here!

With our eyes directed toward Christ, whether we are physically weakened or enjoying health, we all have opportunities to demonstrate our devotion to Him through service. Please remember: prayer, encouraging calls, visits, and notes are valuable ways to serve. Every few months, I receive a note in the mail—yes, snail mail—from a woman I've known almost three decades. I rarely cross physical paths with her, but she is faithful to let me know she is praying for me and always sends me an encouraging scripture. Each time I open one of these thoughtful envelopes, I feel the load lighten just a bit, and I'm reminded to keep forging ahead.

I am always encouraged to hear of my friends who are older than I am—some in their nineties—who are still excited to share truth with those around them. They are able to speak, so they are serving.

One of the aging ladies I am blessed to know has been hospitalized several times as she is physically declining. However, when she is in the hospital, she takes every opportunity to share the truth of God's love with those around her.

Often, we have opportunities to serve right within our families. And something we can always do is pray. I love it when I know people are praying for me!

So we may be decaying on the outside, but we can expect to continually be strengthened on the inside, in our souls, which will live forever. In sickness and in health, we can be faithful to serve the one who gave all for us.

Colossians 3:1–3 says, "If then you have been raised up with Christ, keep seeking the things above, where Christ is, seated at the right hand of God. Set your mind on the things above, not on the things that are on earth. For you have died and your life is hidden with Christ in God."

CHAPTER 6

Hand in Hand

To Love and to Cherish

Is there anyone who doesn't want to be loved and cherished? Those words are included in wedding vows written hundreds of years ago and are still used today, so someone must have thought they were important. I found this definition of human love in a dictionary: "An intense feeling of tender affection; something that elicits deep interest and enthusiasm in somebody."

Included in the same definition were these phrases: "The mercy, grace, and charity shown by God to humanity" and "The worship and adoration of God." To love someone or something carries the meaning of devotion. *Even to a largely unsaved world, love is often equated with God.*

The words *mercy, grace,* and *charity* are worth looking at a bit closer. Mercy is showing leniency and compassion toward someone who has offended you. It displays a quality of being kind and forgiving. Years ago I learned an acrostic for grace—God's Riches at Christ's Expense. This is a significant thought and it's biblically true. God's riches means all the blessings He continually bestows upon us; Christ's expense means He paid the penalty of our sin, which allows us to have a meaningful relationship with God. Charity is typically associated with certain groups that promote public welfare. It has at its core a kind and loving attitude toward those in need.

The world does have an understanding and grasp of love. And even the way we define some of these terms sounds right. Perhaps the most significant difference between God's love toward us and our love toward Him and others is that we fail and He does not. In fact, God cannot fail. His execution of love is perfect, without flaw, and completely unconditional in its delivery. God's love is independent of our actions.

How difficult is it to love someone who is either unresponsive to your care or treats you unkindly? Unconditional love is extremely hard for us to maintain for lengthy periods of time.

The word *cherish* is not often used in our everyday language. Yet we all have people, memories, and things that we cherish. They are the things that have value to us even though their value may not be recognized by another.

For instance, we cherish a moment of affection from a child or a special interaction with a friend or loved one. When we cherish something, there is usually a sentiment attached that gives it value, most often a memory.

My husband lived in a rural area many years ago. On his property, he had a very large workshop, where he kept many of his dad's tools and some personal items his dad had given him over the years. A fire swept through the area and burned down all the trees as well as his workshop and everything in it. My husband was thankful the house was untouched and no one was injured; however, it was difficult for him to lose his dad's old pocket watch. He valued that watch because he had memories of his dad carrying it with him. It had no monetary value but was loved and cherished by my husband.

I host Thanksgiving at my home every two years. I always look forward to using the same dish I remember my grandmother putting on the table with cranberry sauce in it. It's actually chipped a bit on the edge, but I use it anyway because it means something to me—I cherish the sentiment it evokes.

When we have a deep interest or enthusiasm for something, the people around us know. We value it, we remember it, and we speak highly of it. When we love and cherish God, we are led to honor His name through our obedience to His Word.

These days, I am blessed with several toddler-age grandchildren, all of whom I get to spend time with. Each of them, when they are corrected by their parents, show absolute remorse because they hurt Mommy and Daddy in their disobedience. Picture two little eyes filled with tears and the words "I'm sorry" coming out of their mouths.

There is no question of God's continued love and care for His children. God will remain faithful to those He has called even when they walk away. Look at the example we have in the nation of Israel. They left the God who had chosen them, yet He remained faithful to His promises.

God is for you! Is your life about Him? What is your evidence?

Colossians 3:3 says, "For you have died and your life is hidden with Christ in God." Galatians 2:20 states, "I have been crucified with Christ; and it is no longer I who live, but Christ lives in me; and the life which I now live in the flesh I live by faith in the Son of God, who loved me, and delivered Himself up for me."

Obedience and serving go hand in hand. These are actions that show our love for Christ. To cherish what is valuable is the example we have been given in Jesus's life.

Matthew 20:28 tells us, "The Son of Man did not come to be served, but to serve, and to give His life as a ransom for many." In obedience to His Father, Jesus laid down His life for us.

When we love and cherish someone, we are obedient to them. We dutifully comply with their commands and instructions. We place ourselves in a position of submission under their authority. *Because we want to.* We willingly give up any ownership we have claimed for our lives and look to live for Christ so that He might be honored.

Before anyone accepts Jesus as their Savior, they have their roots dug deep into the world and are controlled by sin. We are born with a sinful nature. To understand this, watch a couple of two- and three-year-olds for a moment. Their lives are about them and pretty much anything done is to serve self because that's what is known.

When someone's life is changed by God's grace and he or she accepts His gift of eternal life, that person becomes dead to sin's control. Obedience to God, rather than self and sin, begins to characterize the person's life.

From the moment of salvation and into eternity, a true believer lives for Jesus—the focus and the purpose of life is to bring glory to Him. This is done by striving to live by His Word. The object of their love is God. Obedience to His Word becomes a heartfelt desire.

Can we do this perfectly? Oh my goodness, no! But because of God's grace, we can pursue a life of purity and give obedience a monumental effort. When we mess up and take our eyes off the truth, we confess and turn back around from sin. We do not stay there! We are no longer controlled by sin's power.

We are reminded by the Holy Spirit how to live, and we are given understanding of God's truths. We can rely upon God's strength in our lives to help us avoid living a life characterized by sin.

1 Corinthians 2:12–13 reads, "Now we have received, not the spirit of the world, but the Spirit who is from God, that we might know the things freely given to us by God, which things we also speak, not in words taught by human wisdom, but in those taught by the Spirit, combining spiritual thoughts with spiritual words."

After Paul's conversion, it is written in Acts 18:5 that Paul "began devoting himself completely to the word." This same scripture in the King James Version says, "Paul was pressed in the spirit." Paul was preoccupied; he was constrained to speak of Jesus.

Many years ago, a movie named *Nanny McPhee* was released. There is one part of the movie I recall. It's at the climax of the entire story when the dad is standing at the altar ready to be married to a woman who strongly dislikes his children.

Not long before this scene, the kids were quite unruly, hence the need for a nanny. Through Nanny McPhee's care, the children had learned to obey. As a result, when they are told to behave by their future stepmom, they do take her seriously. In this scene, they look to their beloved nanny to save the day and stop the wedding. She simply winks, reminds them they need to behave, and then tells them they'll think of a way out.

As the youngest child mutters the word *behave* over and over, the children suddenly hear the sound of buzzing bees. They soon catch on to the same idea as they all begin faking bee attacks, swatting the air and mimicking buzzing sounds. In case you have not seen the movie, I will not give the ending away, but I will make an illustration out of it relating to our own obedience to God.

We may not always understand the circumstances God allows in our lives. We may not get answers to the questions we have. But that's okay. God knows all things. He has power over all things. He simply asks us to obey Him. It's His job to keep us on our feet as He sees fit. He'll show us how and when to change direction if needed, and He'll provide the events that are necessary to bring about change and His blessings. We just need to bee-have!

We know God loves us. Our willingness to obey shows our love for Him. And we are blessed as He guides us on a straight path when we obey. We are blessed by avoiding some major mishaps in our lives.

Several years ago, when my dad was still on this earth, my parents were visiting and offered to take me out to dinner. We drove to a restaurant, and my dad parked the car. Because it looked busy, my mom quickly got out of the vehicle and went ahead of us to put our name on the waiting list.

As she hurried across the parking lot toward the entrance of the building, she failed to see the curb directly in front of her. She tripped and fell hard onto the asphalt. My dad and I had just begun walking toward the entrance when we saw her fall. My dad of course began running to help her. In his panic, he tripped over the same curb and landed directly on top of my mom! It looked like they were playing a game of human dominoes. It's okay to laugh at this story because they both ended up being just fine. They were a bit embarrassed, and we shared a chuckle as we ate our meal.

When we desire God to direct our path and we follow Him in obedience, we are blessed by His help in avoiding the obstacles we may not see, which cause us to trip and fall as we navigate through this world.

We are devoted to God because we love Him. Loving God leads us to obey His Word. Obedience to God leads us to serving Him through others. But what does serving out of obedience look like? How can we tell if we are serving self or others?

Who benefits most? Whose interests am I more concerned with?

Read Paul's words as he explains our Christian service in Romans 12:10–18:

> Be devoted to one another in brotherly love; give
> preference to one another in honor; not lagging

behind in diligence, fervent in spirit, serving the Lord; rejoicing in hope, persevering in tribulation, devoted to prayer, contributing to the needs of the saints, practicing hospitality. Bless those who persecute you; bless and curse not. Rejoice with those who rejoice, and weep with those who weep. Be of the same mind toward one another; do not be haughty in mind, but associate with the lowly. Do not be wise in your own estimation. Never pay back evil for evil to anyone. Respect what is right in the sight of all men. If possible, so far as it depends on you, be at peace with all men.

To practically love and cherish God means we will show our devotion to Him by choosing to follow His commands. We serve Him by serving others. Valuing God's Word means we will strive to remember what it says. Our love for God will permeate our thoughts and show in our actions and in our words.

We are loved and cherished. God shows us an abundance of mercy and compassion. He extends grace to all who will receive it. Our acts of serving show our love and gratitude toward God for what we've been given through His Son.

In this book, I've used what would be thought of as traditional wedding vows and have proposed the application of them to God's love and commitment toward us, and our commitment to Christ when we, through grace, accept Him as our Lord and Savior.

Before we go on to the next chapter, we should recap what has been previously covered. Keep in mind the relation of what God has done for us through His Son, our acceptance of His gift, His commitment of love toward us, and our act of obedience toward Him with a heart of gratitude.

In chapter 1, I replaced the words "I take," typically heard at the beginning of wedding vows, with "I confess." This is significant! We do not bring anything to God. Because of His grace, He offers us everything! The word *take* implies that a union is by my choice. The word *confess* means we admit and agree to our need of a Savior, and God's choosing us!

"I confess You, Jesus Christ, are God, that You became flesh, lived as man and died for my sins. I receive You as my Lord and Savior."

In chapter 2, the words "to have and to hold from this day forward" speak of our security in Christ. Therefore, we can say emphatically, "No one will be able to snatch me out of Your hands, and I will be known as Your child forever."

Chapter 3 reviews the phrase "for better or for worse" and causes us to have a deeper understanding of blessings in good times and in trials. "As Your child, I am a recipient of Your abundant blessings; I will also expect loving discipline from You as my heavenly Father."

The fourth chapter explored the application of the words "for richer or poorer."

(For richer): "I will rejoice in times of prosperity and blessing while keeping my focus and purpose on the one true treasure which is eternal life."

(For poorer): "I will rejoice and prevail in times of need and will look to You for al things, remembering You are the source of all blessings and all I could eve want is found in You alone".

We are to rejoice in times of prosperity and blessing while keeping our focus and purpose on loving and serving God, awaiting the treasure of eternal life.

We are to rejoice in times of need and difficulty, looking to God to supply all things. God alone is the source of our hearts' desire, and everything we need is found in Him.

On to chapter 5 and the words, "In sickness and in health." Here, we took a close look at our understanding of God's faithfulness in every season. His example leads our focus to remain on Him and our service to be strong for Him, even when it is difficult. "Whether I am struggling with physical illness and weakness or enjoying wellness and energy, I will look to each day as an opportunity to prove my faith as I remain focused and bent on serving You in whatever way I am able. I will hold on to Your strength and the guidance of Your Spirit and will expect to flourish even in the most difficult times."

The words "to love and to cherish" begin chapter 6. Our rewritten phrase now says, "I will love and cherish You and will demonstrate this by my obedience to You. I will honor Your name above all else, seeking to glorify You in every situation."

We love and cherish God because we understand who He is and what He has done. This understanding leads to a thankful heart and the motivation for our service becomes gratitude. The purpose of our lives is to bring glory and honor to His name.

CHAPTER 7

Purity and Devotion

Forsaking All Others, Keeping Myself Only unto You

Wedding vows have been recited for centuries between two individuals who plan to devote themselves to each other. Seeing that the church is referred to as Christ's bride in the Bible, I have appropriated these vows to our relationship with Jesus Christ as our Lord and Savior.

What does His relationship to His children look like? Jesus loves us—that is why He laid down His life. He offers to us a proposal—the gift of salvation. When we accept this gift, He claims us as His own and gives us the Holy Spirit as a guide. He stays with us through the easy blessings and the blessings that are not so much fun, the ones that stretch and grow our dependence and trust in Him. We can lean on His strength when things get tough. He is 100 percent committed to His children's welfare.

Are we committed to Christ? Are we willing to live our lives completely for His glory?

Revelation 19:7 says, "Let us rejoice and be glad and give the glory to Him, for the marriage of the Lamb has come and His bride has made herself ready."

The truth of our future is incredibly exciting! Read Revelation 21:1–2: "And I saw a new heaven and a new earth; for the first heaven and the first earth passed away, and there is no longer [any] sea. And I saw the holy city, new Jerusalem, coming down out of heaven from God, made ready as a bride adorned for her husband."

Remember what Jesus has done for us so that we might anticipate the promise of eternal life we have through Him. Ephesians 5:25–27 reads, "Husbands, love your wives, just as Christ also loved the church and gave Himself up for her; that He might sanctify her, having cleansed her by the washing of water with the word, that He might present to Himself the church in all her glory, having no spot or wrinkle or any such thing; but that she should be holy and blameless."

The truths written for us in God's Word point toward our purpose—that we might one day be in His presence. Until that time, we are called to live solely for Him, keeping our eyes on His truths and our future.

When we dropped our oldest son off at college, it was difficult leaving him thousands of miles away. We loaded him up with phone cards (cell phones were not as available then) and learned, like so many parents have done in the past, to trust that God would use the truths that our son had heard to guide him and keep him safe.

We did have computers, so I wrote often to our son, and it was then that I began signing my notes with the words "Focus heavenward." Those two words were my strength and purpose, and I knew they would guide our son in his decisions as he looked to God.

It's not always easy to look closely at ourselves and our struggles and weaknesses. Many times we fall short. Our failures can sometimes flash back at us like bright neon signs. However, there is encouragement! God will not change His mind about the love He has given us. He accepts even our smallest offerings of service. He knows we are weak. Remember, He is our Savior—that title implies our great need!

What God desires from us is our hearts and our complete devotion.

Often, traditional wedding vows include the phrase "Forsaking all others, keeping myself only unto you." When we forsake someone or something, we withdraw. Forsaking means to leave one thing for another, to give something up.

This is an important concept when we realize the sin nature we have. Before the understanding of God's grace was bestowed upon us, we lived for what we thought was best. Now, living for Christ, our motivation changes to what God says is best: a giving up of self for Him. We need to remove those things that tempt us to set God aside and replace them with the people and things that draw our devotion toward Him.

What pulls you from your relationship with Christ?

We can easily become distracted by the things around us; we forget that while we may live on this earth, our citizenship is in heaven. Philippians 3:20 says, "For our citizenship is in heaven, from which also we eagerly wait for a Savior, the Lord Jesus Christ."

The promise of our lives with Christ should point our affections *toward* God and *away* from the things in this world, as we look forward to our future in God's kingdom. This truth causes us to have joy from within as our hearts are drawn to our true treasure!

Think of planning a trip. First, a destination is chosen. Then you might think of the details about how you get there. At one point, you begin to pack the clothing and things you will need. Often, maps are looked at and time schedules are decided upon. All the while, excitement builds as you prepare, and you find your thoughts gravitating toward your future plans. Anticipation motivates you as you get closer and closer to arriving at your destination. While eagerly awaiting your trip, more and more of your time, energy, and thoughts go into preparation.

God is already preparing for His children's arrival!

John 14:2 tell us this very thing: "In My Father's house are many dwelling places; if it were not so, I would have told you; for I go to prepare a place for you."

Are we devoted to preparing ourselves for Him, forsaking the things that draw our attention away? If we are honest, we realize we can say with our words that we are devoted to God alone, but the world has quite a pull in many different areas. Do our actions speak of our devotion to God? Do our thoughts remain steadfast on His truths?

We want things the world offers, and we want what God says—our affections and our devotion need to be settled in only one place. We are blessed by having so much available to us, yet we are also challenged constantly to keep our focus on the things that are not of this earth.

Earlier, I addressed some of the more difficult times in our lives: times when God allows trials for the purpose of discipline, times of struggle and need, and times of physical weakness and illness. In all these situations, as well as when things are going well, we are to put God first—in every circumstance, at any cost.

2 Timothy 4:2 tells us to "preach the word; be ready in season and out of season." This scripture says to proclaim Jesus when the opportunity is convenient and likewise when it is inconvenient, even when there are obstructions or hindrances. In fact, if you back up to the first verse of 2 Timothy 4, you will read that this is a charge to us, not a suggestion.

2 Timothy 4:1 says, "I solemnly charge [you] in the presence of God and of Christ Jesus, who is to judge the living and the dead, and by His appearing and His kingdom."

Several years ago, our son and his wife were stationed at an air force base in Florida. While we were visiting, we attended a Sunday service at their church. The sermon topic was on witnessing, and there was a newsletter included in the bulletin entitled "Glimpses" that highlighted people, events, life, and faith from the church across the ages. It was published by the Christian History Institute.

This pamphlet had an article about George Whitefield, a controversial evangelist born in the 1700s. He was considered controversial because he "refused to soft-pedal his preaching. His bluntness sometimes offended people." The article said that George Whitefield detested lukewarm Christianity. "To him, it was worse than no faith at all … he made every effort to shake churchgoers out of their apathy." He reminded his listeners of "the church at Laodicea in Revelation 3:16, where Christ said He would spew such congregations out of His mouth. The only kind of faith that pleased God was fervent, heartfelt belief."

Wouldn't you have loved to have been at one of his sermons!

Read this quote from Albert *Barnes' New Testament Commentary*:

> A man who is greatly intent on an object will seek every opportunity to promote it. He will not confine himself to stated times and places, but will present it everywhere, and at all times.

A man, therefore, who merely confines himself to the stated seasons of preaching the gospel, or who merely reaches when it is convenient to himself, should not consider that he has come up to the requirement of the rule laid down by the apostle (Paul). He should preach in his private conversation, and in the intervals of his public labours, at the side of the sick bed, and wherever there is a prospect of doing good to anyone. *If his heart is full of love to the Savior and to souls, he cannot help doing this.* (emphasis mine)

That's what you call devotion: putting God first, forsaking all else!

In John 4:34, Jesus says, "My food is to do the will of Him who sent Me, and to accomplish His work."

Job, even amid his suffering, claimed, "I have not departed from the command of His lips; I have treasured the words of His mouth more than my necessary food" (Job 23:12).

Did you catch the use of the word *food* in the above scripture? Food is necessary for growth. Food sustains our lives. Without it, we would starve. Starvation is a severe form of malnutrition. According to *The Free Dictionary by Farlex*, total starvation is fatal in eight to twelve weeks.

Are you devoted to a steady diet in God's Word, or are you starving, barely taking enough in to keep you alive?

An important part of being devoted to Jesus is setting the priority to spend time with Him by reading the Bible and praying and asking God to search your heart, to give you understanding, and to show you how to apply the truths He so graciously has preserved. If you are saved, God in His goodness and mercy has chosen you.

Isn't it reasonable to presume that we would make a deliberate decision to get to know Him by spending concentrated time with Him?

We cannot put God in a box and check it off; He's always with us throughout each moment. We need to spend time with God, presenting to Him an unhurried and uncluttered heart, mind, and soul without distraction just as we would do for anything or anyone we are truly interested in.

The advance of technology has opened many opportunities of communication. It has also become an easy distraction. While on vacation, my husband and I stopped in a small bakery for lunch. There were several tables with couples, individuals, and families gathered round. I noticed what appeared to be a family of four sitting near us. Throughout our entire meal, we watched the two adults and two teenage children accomplish eating lunch together without sharing a single spoken word. They were connected the entire time to their personal phones, either texting or gaming or listening to music with earbuds. There was no verbal form of communication between them. They were certainly in one another's presence, but they had not spent any time with one another at all.

How can we truly show our love and devotion to others without listening and hearing and speaking and showing an interest in who they are, what they like, what they want, and what's important to them?

Spending time with God is essential in our relationship with Him. How else are we going to be prepared in season and out of season to share His glorious truths to those around us? How else are we going to be able to navigate through a difficult and sometimes treacherous climb?

Devotion to God is a constant commitment to Him, a dedication to follow His ways. It is not just grazing when we run out of energy or need encouragement. Or gorging ourselves at one time then starving ourselves at another. To be dedicated to God means we show our allegiance to Him; we are loyal. And we look forward to unhurried time in His presence, soaking up who He is and what He desires us to be for Him.

In a marriage, it is expected that fidelity to each other will be practiced. Keeping a marriage relationship pure by having eyes only for each other is part of showing one's complete devotion and commitment.

The way we use our time speaks of our commitment to God.

In Luke 1:75, we read that we are to live "in holiness and righteousness before Him all our days." *All* of them, not just some of them or most of them. We do not seek God on Sunday and then claim the rest of the week as our own. If this is our practice, we are in danger of malnutrition!

When you take a vacation, do you vacate God? Who purposed that you would be able to enjoy time away from your normal routine?

I pray that if we are blessed to be able to set aside the pressures of commitments for a short time, this does not include abandoning God! God is not a responsibility that we take care of. God is our reason for living. In fact, our times away for refreshment should be centered on the anticipation of spending *more* precious moments with our Savior.

Romans 14:6–8 tells us, "He who observes the day, observes it for the Lord, and he who eats, does so for the Lord, for he gives thanks to God; and he who eats not, for the Lord he does not eat, and gives thanks to God. For not one of us lives for himself, and not one dies for himself; for if we live, we live for the Lord, or if we die, we die for the Lord; therefore whether we live or die, we are the Lord's."

In whatever we do, we are to be devoted to God, we are to remain pure in Him and live for Him. We are to bring glory and honor to Him in all things.

1Corinthians 10:31 says, "Whether, then, you eat or drink or whatever you do, do all to the glory of God."

Joshua reminds us of the choice we need to make. Read Joshua 24:15: "And if it is disagreeable in your sight to serve the LORD, choose for yourselves today whom you will serve: whether the gods which your fathers served which were beyond the river, or the gods of the Amorites in whose land you are living; but as for me and my house, we will serve the LORD."

One of the first things I did when we moved into the house we now live in was to stencil the words "As for me and my house, we will serve the Lord" at the top of the doorway molding in the entry. Each time I walk through the entry, I am reminded whose house I live in. I am only a steward of what God has given me. Being a steward means I am to manage it wisely. I always need this reminder, or I can easily make decisions without regard to what God would have me do. The same goes for the time we have, the material possessions we have, the children we may have, the spouses we may have, our friends, our neighbors, our abilities, and so on. In all of these things, we are to be devoted to knowing and showing God's truths.

Ephesians 5:27 tells us that God loves us and is waiting to present us "to Himself as a radiant church, without stain or wrinkle or any other blemish, but holy and blameless."

There was a time when my husband and I would go out to lunch each Sunday after church. Our oldest son was married and living out of state and our two youngest were away at college, so it was just the two of us. One such time, we decided to try a new place that had opened, which served mostly barbeque. We ordered our lunch and were enjoying the delicious food. Having six different sauces to try at the table proved to be a fun experiment.

I found my favorite and picked up the squeeze bottle full of this sauce called "sweet and zesty." I gave the bottle a hefty squeeze and almost the entire contents exploded out onto the white skirt and lilac-colored shirt I was wearing! My hair, face, arm, blouse, and skirt were covered in rich, red sauce.

Take a moment and form a clear mental picture of this in your mind, and you will have the complete opposite of our presentation to Christ without stain or blemish!

Because of our union with Him, we are justified, sanctified, and will one day be glorified as we are presented to Him pure and undefiled. This is opposite of what I did as I was walking out of the restaurant. I walked as close as possible behind my husband, hoping no one would see me!

Christ paid for our sin, He took our shame upon Himself. We have been cleansed from within, our very souls are seen pure and spotless when we accept His sacrifice. The Bible says God looks at our hearts. I think we can conclude that the most important characteristic of people who are godly is their obvious love for the Lord, which is evident in their devotion to Him.

Despite circumstances of our lives on this earth that disappoint us and the heartaches we may experience, we are to remain faithful to God. Our choices and actions should honor His name.

Times of uncertainty or when we feel let down by another should turn us toward God, seeking His perfect instruction, not away from Him.

In Joshua 1:16, we read, "Whatever You have commanded us we will do, and wherever You send us we will go." May that be the commitment of God's children.

The devotion to God in the Macedonia church is recorded for us in 2 Corinthians 8:1–5:

> Now, brethren, we [wish to] make known to you the grace of God which has been given in the churches of Macedonia, that in a great ordeal of affliction their abundance of joy and their deep poverty overflowed in the wealth of their liberality. For I testify that according to their ability, and beyond their ability [they gave] of their own accord, begging us with much entreaty for

the favor of participation in the support of the
saints, and [this,] not as we had expected, but they
first gave themselves to the Lord and to us by the
will of God.

Notice that the Macedonian Christians first honored God
by the giving of themselves to Him. We need to be dedicated to
honoring God with our whole lives—our time, efforts, resources,
and abilities—anything He requires of us. And not only when it
is convenient for us or enjoyable. All we have is from Him and is
to be used for Him.

I, like you, have struggled with putting God first sometimes. I
have to put effort into forsaking all the things that seem to scream
at me for my attention. I recall the many times I have been in the
middle of reading my Bible and studying when the phone rang
and I chose to answer it. Or I allowed the buzzing of my clothes
dryer to draw me away from what was truly important. Or my
mind would begin to wander into thinking of all the things that
needed to get done that day. There have even been times when
I just wanted to finish reading so that I could pursue the latest
creative interest I had.

In those times, I certainly do not have my complete focus
on God. My attention is divided, and I am offering to God my
leftovers or only pieces of myself. Does this speak of whole-heart
devotion?

Most of us would not think of leaving the house without
brushing our teeth, but we have left the house without reading
and praying, without feeding our souls.

Perhaps you make time for exercise, which is important, but
is it at the expense of spending personal time with God? Our
priorities say a lot about what is most important to us. As I stated, I
was convicted by my choices of letting things distract me. I began
turning everything off that could be a distraction. Praise God, for
many years now, I have been able to enjoy a quiet time with no

influences pulling me away or causing my attention to be divided. In fact, as I have tried to remain faithful, God has blessed me by increasing my appetite for Him.

I remember a television show called *What Not to Wear*. The hosts ambush an unsuspecting person to point out all his or her fashion blunders. At the beginning of the show, the person they approach has to agree to give him- or herself over "mind, body and clothes."

The key here is the necessity to give *everything* over, allowing the hosts to sort through all the clothing, throwing out what they do not like. Then the person must follow the guideline set by his or her personal fashion designers in choosing a new wardrobe, including hairstyle and makeup. I'm laughing to myself as I write this because right now I am wearing jeans that are too big, a wrinkled fuchsia-and-black-checked flannel shirt, a navy-and-light-blue hoodie, black socks, and gray slippers. I have showered and my hair is washed but not fixed; I am wearing no makeup; and it's almost three o'clock in the afternoon. It's too bad they missed such a great opportunity!

Anyway, once the bewildered person agrees to the rules, he or she is handed a credit card with $5,000 on it. (Just a side note, I would most definitely have participated!) Some of the transformations truly are remarkable. The individuals revealed at the end of the program usually looked quite different than they did at the beginning. And often their personalities seemed to gain a new sparkle!

Our whole beings need to be devoted to Christ:

- our hearts—our feelings, intuitions, emotions, character, and affections
- our minds—including our ideas, perceptions, intellect, judgments, and reasoning
- our souls—our cores, the embodiment of our consciousness and very beings

When we are completely devoted to Christ, we learn to trust Him as He transforms us. We become less of self and more of Jesus. I'm sure many of you are able to look back several years ago and see change in your thinking and behavior. I seriously do not even recognize who I was decades ago; I truly am completely changed by God's grace, and He's not done with me yet (thankfully!).

Keeping ourselves wholly devoted to God requires more than just lip service; it is our life service.

Most of us are fairly adept at lip service, sharing what we think should be done. But action needs to follow. The best intentions mean nothing if they aren't carried out.

James 2:17–18 says, "Even so faith, if it has no works, is dead, [being] by itself. But someone may well say, "You have faith, and I have works; show me your faith without the works, and I will show you my faith by my works."

Read also James 2:26: "For just as the body without [the] spirit is dead, so also faith without works is dead."

Lawrence Richards's *The Teacher's Commentary* says, "Knowing the Bible is not the key—applying what God has revealed in our daily lives is what counts. Knowing what we should do is not enough—it is putting what we know into practice to live a life worthy of God."

Lord, help us to forsake all things contrary to Your truth, keeping ourselves fully committed to You as our heavenly Father. In purity and devotion, give us eyes and hearts only for You.

CHAPTER 8

Face-to-Face

Until Death Do We Meet

Hasn't this been fun! I had to write those words. Let me explain. After leading a women's Bible study for many years, some of the ladies presented me with a shirt embroidered with the words, "Isn't This Fun?" I did not realize I said those words repeatedly when speaking of God's truths and their application to our lives. Well, it is fun! I pray you have felt my excitement about God's love for you in this book. We truly have a treasure in the words God has written for His children. The Bible is the most important manual for life you will ever read, and it is 100 percent without error. There is nothing that even comes close to who God is and what He has done for us. Get excited about His love for you and His commitment to you!

We have reached the last section of our rewritten wedding vows! I pray you are encouraged and challenged in your commitment to our Lord, Jesus Christ, just as I have been while writing this.

A vow is a pledge to another person to do something or to behave in a certain manner. It is a promise.

There are many vows that we traditionally hold in place. Think of the vows or oaths taken in medical school upon becoming a doctor or in law school when graduating. A pledge is made to uphold certain values that have been put into place to act a certain way when practicing your newfound position.

Vows are like contracts—in most cases we are held accountable to the pledges we take. There is a difference, however, in the promises we have from God and the promises we make or have from people. People are imperfect; therefore, we see promises broken all around us. The value of a handshake, for instance, is not what it used to be. In general, today a handshake is merely a greeting. But it originated as a seal of agreement. When deciding upon a trade in business ventures, a handshake long ago was like having a signature witnessed by a notary public today.

Now, in almost every agreement made—business, political, or social—there are so many papers that require signatures and initials, along with words and explanations that are difficult to understand and written in legalese, that our simple handshake has lost value. Reasons for not keeping our promises are too easily excused away.

Not so with God. What He says, He does. You've heard the saying that someone's word is as good as gold? It means it is reliable, it is genuine, it is authentic, and it is legitimate. In other words, you can trust in it. Well, God's Word is better than gold! Why? Because we can trust in His words completely. God does not change. He is immutable. There are several references in His Word that support this truth.

For instance, the first part of Malachi 3:6 says, "For I, the Lord, do not change." And Hebrews 13:8 states, "Jesus Christ [is] the same yesterday and today, [yes] and forever." One of my favorite scriptures in James reads, "Every good thing bestowed and every perfect gift is from above, coming down from the Father of lights, with whom there is no variation, or shifting shadow" (James 1:17).

Sometimes, before we pledge our allegiance to something or someone, we might look at their track record. With God, there is no need to even keep a track record. He is perfect!

Many people today do their shopping online. An important consideration in deciding on some larger items are the reviews available. Good reviews encourage the buyer to purchase; poor reviews cause the potential buyer to look elsewhere. God has no bad reviews from those who are His children. The only negative statements come from those who are unwilling to accept His grace shown toward them.

God is unchangeable in His character. He does not change as the years go on. He does not become forgetful. He cannot be broken. His values do not become modified as He learns new information. He knows and understands everything perfectly, from before time through eternity.

Read the following section of scripture found in the book of Hebrews:

> In the same way God, desiring even more to show to the heirs of the promise the unchangeableness of His purpose, interposed with an oath, in order that by two unchangeable things, in which it is impossible for God to lie, we may have strong encouragement, we who have fled for refuge in laying hold of the hope set before us. This hope

> we have as an anchor of the soul, a [hope] both
> sure and steadfast and one which enters within the
> veil, where Jesus has entered as a forerunner for
> us, having become a high priest forever according
> to the order of Melchizedek. (Hebrews 6:17–20)

We have the promise of life, a certain hope that is unchanging, from God in Christ Jesus (see also 2 Timothy 1:1). We are to persevere in our walk with God, looking to His promise to us as we put all our efforts into our calling as His children.

Hebrews 10:35–38 states, "Therefore, do not throw away your confidence, which has a great reward. For you have need of endurance, so that when you have done the will of God, you may receive what was promised. For yet in a very little while, he who is coming will come, and will not delay. But my righteous one shall live by faith; and if he shrinks back, my soul has no pleasure in him."

The promise I can make to God to live worthy of His calling is only because of the fulfillment of His promises to me as His child in Jesus Christ. In the strength of His might, I am able to walk in faithfulness, fully devoted to the God I love.

(I take you): I confess You, Jesus Christ, are God, that You became flesh, lived as man, and died for my sins.

(To be my lawfully wedded husband/wife): I receive You as my Savior and Lord.

(To have and to hold from this day forward): No one will be able to snatch me out of Your hands, and I will be known as Your child forever.

(For better or for worse): As Your child, I am a recipient of Your abundant blessings; I will also expect loving discipline from You as my heavenly Father.

(For richer): I will rejoice in times of prosperity and blessing while keeping my focus and purpose on the one true treasure, which is eternal life.

(For poorer): I will rejoice and prevail in times of need and will look to You for all things, remembering You are the source of all blessings and all I could ever want is found in You alone.

(In sickness and in health): Whether I am struggling with physical illness and weakness or enjoying a time of physical wellness and energy, I will look to each as an opportunity to prove my faith as I remain focused and bent on serving You in whatever way I am able. I will hold on to Your strength and the guidance of Your Spirit and will expect to flourish even in the most difficult times.

(To love and to cherish): I will love and cherish You and will demonstrate this by my obedience to You. I will honor Your name above all else, seeking to glorify You in every situation.

(Forsaking all others, keeping myself only unto You): I will remain true to You in mind, heart, and soul, choosing loyalty to You over anything or anyone.

(Until death do we part): Until death do we meet and You call me home!

Our rewritten vows end with the words "until death do we meet." This is definitely the most exciting part of this study! This phrase points us toward heaven.

We have an amazing future ahead of us! Colossians 3:4 says: "When Christ, Who is our life, is revealed, then you also will be revealed with Him in glory."

Without Christ, we are spiritually dead. As believers, Christ is our life. His Spirit lives in us and our lives are lived for Him. Earlier, I referenced Galatians 2:20, which says, "I have been crucified with Christ; and it is no longer I who live, but Christ lives in me; and the life which I now live in the flesh I live by faith in the Son of God, who loved me, and delivered Himself up for me."

Those who have accepted Jesus as their Lord and Savior have been given the gift of heaven. It is certain. Our relationship with Him is forever. Romans 8:35 presents a rhetorical question: "Who shall separate us from the love of Christ? Shall tribulation, or distress, or persecution, or famine, or nakedness, or peril, or sword?"

Many are familiar with the answer to that question in Romans 8:38–39: "For I am convinced that neither death, nor life, nor angels, nor principalities, nor things present, nor things to come, nor powers, nor height, nor depth, nor any other created thing, shall be able to separate us from the love of God, which is in Christ Jesus our Lord."

The months of preparation needed to plan some weddings all focus on that one special day. Every decision is made with the great expectation of uniting two people in a covenant that will last until one of them dies.

We have Christ's promise of a future beyond death. He will be waiting for us when He calls us home and redeems the church as His bride.

Isaiah 62:5 says that as "the bridegroom rejoices over the bride, so your God will rejoice over you." We are being prepared, as heirs of Christ, to live in His kingdom forever!

In John 17:24, Jesus says, "Father, I desire that they also, whom Thou hast given Me, be with Me where I am, in order that they may behold My glory, which Thou hast given Me."

Upon our deaths on this earth, we will truly be home. As children of God, we await the presentation of His church at the most glorious wedding in the history of the world. Our home will be a perfect kingdom of divine glory that we are simply unable to comprehend while living on this earth.

I found an article in a wedding magazine that posed the question, "What could be grander than a castle wedding? Complete with spectacular grounds, formal banquet halls, and antique-appointed bedrooms, these luxurious estates offer a great way to indulge your inner fairy princess in royal fashion."

What could be grander than a castle wedding?

The destination we are headed because of our salvation! Revelation 21 describes the New Jerusalem, God's eternal kingdom: "Its brilliance was like that of a very precious jewel, like jasper, clear as crystal."

The same chapter goes on to describe walls made of jasper and an entire city of pure gold, as pure glass. The foundations of the city walls are decorated with every kind of precious stone. The gates are pearls, the streets are pure gold. The kingdom itself is lit by the glory of God.

How are your preparations for your wedding coming along? How are you doing in your commitment to follow Christ as Lord and Savior?

Both are essential.

o   He is our Savior, having redeemed us from the penalty of sin that separates us from God.
o   He is ourLord, calling us to live in a manner that puts Him first in all things.

A deeper understanding of God's love for you and His commitment to you *will* draw you closer in your devotion to Him. As your obedience and love for God grows, those around you will be blessed and encouraged. Your purpose will center on serving

God and serving others unconditionally. How might this improve your relationships with your spouse, family, friends, coworkers, and church?

I pray your focus is drawn to Christ's eternal kingdom, where you will finally meet your Lord and Savior face-to-face.

Until Death Do We Meet

Then …

I will enter into Your presence for eternity
As Your child, safe and secure.
The recipient of Your greatest blessing,
Refined by Your fire,
Rejoicing in the treasure of life everlasting.
Present in spirit, awaiting a body perfected,
Purified by Your holiness.
Perseverance and obedience rewarded,
The words, "Well done, my good and faithful servant" realized.
Face-to-face with my Lord and Savior,
Bowing down before Your throne,
Praising Your name forevermore.
What a glorious day attained,
Way too marvelous to comprehend.
But because of Your precious blood,
I am granted Your amazing love.

Focus heavenward with me,
Sharyn

NOTES

CPSIA information can be obtained
at www.ICGtesting.com
Printed in the USA
BVHW080845170619
551189BV00002B/333/P